Penguin Specials fill a gap. Written by some of today's most exciting and insightful writers, they are short enough to be read in a single sitting – when you're stuck on a train; in your lunch hour; between dinner and bedtime. Specials can provide a thought-provoking opinion, a primer to bring you up to date, or a striking piece of fiction. They are concise, original and affordable.

To browse digital and print Penguin Specials titles, please refer to **penguin.com.au/penguinspecials**

Penguin Specials fill a gap. Written by some of today's most exciting and insightful writers, they are short enough to be read in a single sitting – when you're stuck on a train, in your lunch hour, between meetings and bedtime. Specials can provide a thought-provoking opinion, a primer to bring you up to date, or a stunning work of fiction. They are concise, original and affordable.

To browse digital and print Penguin Specials titles, please refer to penguin.com.au/penguinspecials

Take Your Best Shot

JACQUELINE KENT

PENGUIN BOOKS

Published by the Penguin Group
Penguin Group (Australia)
707 Collins Street, Melbourne, Victoria 3008, Australia
(a division of Pearson Australia Group Pty Ltd)
Penguin Group (USA) Inc.
375 Hudson Street, New York, New York 10014, USA
Penguin Group (Canada)
90 Eglinton Avenue East, Suite 700, Toronto, Canada ON M4P 2Y3
(a division of Pearson Penguin Canada Inc.)
Penguin Books Ltd
80 Strand, London WC2R 0RL England
Penguin Ireland
25 St Stephen's Green, Dublin 2, Ireland
(a division of Penguin Books Ltd)
Penguin Books India Pvt Ltd
11 Community Centre, Panchsheel Park, New Delhi 110 017, India
Penguin Group (NZ)
67 Apollo Drive, Rosedale, Auckland 0632, New Zealand
(a division of Pearson New Zealand Ltd)
Penguin Books (South Africa) (Pty) Ltd
Rosebank Office Park, Block D, 181 Jan Smuts Avenue, Parktown North, Johannesburg 2196, South Africa
Penguin (Beijing) Ltd
7F, Tower B, Jiaming Center, 27 East Third Ring Road North, Chaoyang District, Beijing 100020, China

Penguin Books Ltd, Registered Offices: 80 Strand, London WC2R 0RL, England

First published by Penguin Group (Australia), 2013

Cover Image (Julia Gillard) by Gary Ramage/Newspix

ISBN: 9780143570561

penguin.com.au

MIX
Paper from responsible sources
FSC® C001695

CONTENTS

INTRODUCTION

As the title of this book indicates, this is an account of Julia Gillard's tenure as Australia's first woman prime minister. As a biographer, my primary focus is on Gillard herself: though there is of course discussion and some analysis of her programs, I leave it to future political historians to properly evaluate her government and its achievements.

I spoke to Julia Gillard for this book at Kirribilli House early in May 2013, about six weeks before the Caucus vote that ended her three years and three days in what the media always calls the 'top job'. It was the fifth time we had had contact, though our first meeting since she became prime minister. For reasons apart from the obvious, this was very different from our previous encounters.

Julia Gillard had always been most reluctant

to have her story told: when I first requested an interview with her as deputy prime minister early in 2009, as I was writing *The Making of Julia Gillard*, her office refused, and they continued refusing. They consented only because those who had known her in her previous life – as a student activist and industrial lawyer – kept requesting her permission to talk about her. Eventually Gillard and her staff realised that this was a bona fide project and that cooperation was probably sensible.

We had three interviews in 2009, and I also accompanied her to a lunch at Melbourne Town Hall where she outlined her education policies. During our private meetings she was invariably polite and attentive, answering precisely the questions I asked her, and volunteering very little. When I told her that I too had gone to Adelaide University, her only reply was, 'Did you?' Though she was friendly, she never invited connection. In that respect – and only in that respect – I imagine it was a little like talking to the Queen. (However, she did unbend enough later to tell me that being interviewed for her biography made her feel a bit like a lab rat.)

The woman I met in May this year was much easier, warmer, friendlier. She was responsive, she laughed easily, she answered questions fully, she volunteered comments. Certainly the 'lab rat' of four years previous had since been thoroughly dissected by people who were much more expert than I, but her change in demeanour was not, I thought, entirely because she was a more practised politician. (I also don't think her greater cheerfulness came from liking the book, flattering though it would be to think so . . . though in any case it's a bit alarming for a biographer if the subject approves of the work.)

That day, Julia Gillard displayed a lightness of spirit that, considering what she was going through, was nothing short of astonishing. I had expected to find a woman who looked tired or anxious, her manner defensive and brittle. After all, she was leading a government whose majority was on a knife edge. Almost every day for three years she'd faced relentless hostility from the Opposition and large sections of the conservative media, including constant calls for her replacement by the man she had deposed in 2010. She had been a lightning rod for misogyny and endured howls of outrage from various quarters about almost every policy she introduced. The pressure of this time, though, had apparently had little physical effect – her skin was still enviably pale and unlined – but she did now wear rather smart tortoiseshell spectacles (which, her minder told me, had their own Twitter account).

Did Gillard's obvious poise and confidence that

day stem from inside knowledge denied to the pollsters and journalists, or her expectation that she and the ALP would win the next election, due on 14 September? That seemed highly unlikely: for weeks the media had been full of doom. There was even the prediction that under Gillard the ALP would suffer their worst electoral defeat since Federation. Perhaps she was feeling the relief that anybody does when they know that soon they can stop doing a grindingly difficult, almost impossible job. But considering her personality, it was more likely that Gillard had dismissed what she called the 'hurly-burly' from her mind, at least temporarily, because her fate and that of her government was in the hands of the voters.

Gillard was often described as hard to read, and very clearly her warmth and charm do hide a deep reserve and a resolve to protect herself. When I commented on this she told me, 'I draw a very hard line in my mind between the public hurly-burly and my sense of myself and who I am. I suspect being able to get a sense of remove on [politics] is a bit like a muscle; the more you work it, the stronger it gets.'

Naturally every politician needs to exercise skills of self-preservation: politicians would not last long if they did not. Yet in Julia Gillard's case there is something more, a resilience and a calm belief in what she did that enabled her to stand up to a relentlessly vicious three-year campaign against her from several quarters.

Nobody develops this kind of strong self-belief from a standing start. Julia Gillard has always made clear that she owes a great deal to her parents, who obviously gave her unconditional love from the very beginning. John and Moira Gillard, both highly intelligent members of mining families in South Wales, had tough early lives, forced by poverty to leave school early and to work in a series of mostly unrewarding jobs. They met and married in Barry, where both were working in the police force, and had two daughters, Alison Mary born in 1958 and Julia Eileen born in 1961. In 1966 when Julia was four, the Gillard family emigrated to Australia as 'ten-pound Poms'. They settled in Adelaide, where John and Moira worked at whatever jobs they could find.

Gillard's birthright included progressive Labor politics. 'We grew up in an environment where we were Labor by instinct,' she said. John and Moira Gillard were great admirers of Aneurin Bevan, the Welsh leader whose legacy includes setting up Britain's National Health Service, and the whole family enthusiastically supported the social policies of Gough Whitlam. The Whitlam government's social democratic agenda undoubtedly influenced Gillard's views about what could be achieved in politics.

Like most migrant families, the Gillards relied very strongly on each other, and their care for each other has continued. 'When the attacks on me [as prime minister] were really nasty a couple of years ago – you know, "ditch the witch" and so on – Dad worried a lot about how I was,' she told me. 'Especially during the protests about carbon pricing, and the so-called people's revolt, he was fearful for me, because he read such an unpleasant edge into the politics.

'But Mum was much more likely to say, Take no notice of them. We know who you are, you know who you are.'

This, said Gillard, was typical of her mother's tough approach to life, and she herself learned from that. 'Mum was never unduly influenced by what other people said. She has always had a very clear sense of who she is.'

Almost from the moment Gillard entered Parliament in 1998 as federal member for the outer Melbourne seat of Lalor, she was a divisive figure. She left a thriving career as an industrial lawyer to run for Parliament, succeeding after five years and two unsuccessful attempts, one to enter the House of Representatives, the other for the Senate. She faced implacable factional opposition at all times, and she succeeded only because she managed to put together a cross-factional deal. Two of her signature qualities – determination and the ability to negotiate – were obvious from the beginning of her political career.

Toughness, being able to go on in the teeth of public opposition, is part of a politician's suit of armour: during her prime ministership, however, Julia Gillard made this into an art form. As columnist Annabel Crabb observed, occasionally it seemed that there was no live grenade upon which the PM was unwilling to launch herself. Certainly effective politicians cannot afford to care about what everybody thinks, but ignoring public opinion is another thing altogether.

As prime minister she was strongly criticised for making judgement calls quickly, without preparing the ground for public acceptance. This led to the perception of policymaking on the run. 'I do try to put efforts and energies into bringing people along with me,' she said. 'I prefer to make our structures work and include people within them to get a say. But it's not possible every day, every time.

'And we can always do better at communicating, though I think sometimes judgements are made without people understanding the context. There's a job for us to be better at conveying what we do, I feel that very keenly.' Many voters would have agreed with her: Gillard's critics might well have argued that it is the PM's job to make sure that voters do understand context.

Undoubtedly because of Gillard's gender, there was a huge concentration on questions of image during her prime ministership. 'There are more complexities about appearance, if you're a woman doing my job, and the first woman doing it . . . I could happily live without that side of it,' she said. 'I've joked with people that most women who pay a lot of attention to their clothing do so because they want other women to comment. I pay endless amounts of attention to it for exactly the opposite reason – I don't want anyone to notice what I wear.

'If I could get that time back and spend it on something else, I cheerfully would.'

A radio journalist friend of mine always asked the cadets she trained for the ABC: Do you want to *be* something, or do you want to *do* something? It's an important question for anyone, perhaps even most significant for a political leader. For Julia Gillard, being prime minister was never an end in itself. She used her power as a tool for problem-solving, which was her real strength: working out ways of achieving what she wanted to do in terms of legislation. In doing this, she probably displayed less sense of occasion than a man would have. I found her informal, even chatty – though when I came to listen back to the interview I realised that, as before, she had given little away. But Gillard appeared to be comfortable with her power. Comfortable enough, anyway, at the end of our meeting, to refer to high-level discussions with the treasurer with the words: 'Well, now I have to go and talk billions with Swanny.'

Walking on eggshells

At the end of the 1998 movie *Elizabeth* Cate Blanchett, as the newly crowned Queen Elizabeth I, reaches for a jar of white makeup and smears it carefully all over her face until her features are hidden behind a calm, expressionless mask. This, the audience is given to understand, symbolises her resolve to put the past, her girlhood, behind her. The person she truly was would henceforth be hidden, if she existed at all. She would be only a public person, a figurehead, the ruler of her country.

It's an image that comes to mind when considering the early days of Julia Gillard's prime ministership in mid 2010.

For three years voters had known her as the warm, unpretentious, and above all competent deputy to prime minister Kevin Rudd. Voters, especially women, liked her. There was endless speculation that she was a prime minister in waiting. She shrugged it all off, saying there was no way she would be Australia's first woman prime minister. And then on the morning of 24 June 2010 the nation discovered that she had become exactly that. Her Caucus colleagues, increasingly dismayed by Rudd's autocratic management style and the stalling of government programs, had asked her to challenge him for the leadership: Rudd chose not to contest the ballot and Gillard won unopposed.

Asked almost three years later about her accession to the prime ministership, Julia Gillard said, 'The events in May and June 2010 had their own momentum. The media said at the time [the impetus to topple Kevin Rudd] was all to do with opinion polls, but it wasn't. It was about a plan of capacity for the future. We were all desperately concerned about where we were as a government and political party, and distressed. We knew we had to do something, things were getting more and more chaotic.

'I don't think, given the circumstances we were in – and I don't want to reflect on how individuals were conducting themselves – we had much choice.'[1]

On that cold June morning, Julia Gillard faced a barrage of journalists who, like the general public, were incredulous, perhaps hostile. In any case, they were looking at her somewhat differently: to most people she had morphed from warm and efficient deputy to ruthless untrustworthy careerist. Facing sceptical journalists, she knew that she had to explain why, in taking over from Kevin Rudd as PM, she had done the right thing.

'It was really quite difficult to tell people what had happened without being disrespectful to Kevin, and I didn't want to do that,' she said. 'That's why I said the government had lost its way. Looking back with hindsight I can see now that this left Australians wondering what was going on, and people sought to fill the void with their own explanations.

'People know much more about what happened now, there have been press stories and even books about it, it's much more transparent.

'However, for anyone to say that my coming to office resulted from the actions of a couple of individuals [the small group of Right-faction powerbrokers who approached her on behalf of the Caucus and who were later stigmatised as the 'faceless men'] is manifestly wrong. It shows that people don't understand the dynamics of Caucus.' At the time an explanation to the public would have been useful: instead Gillard chose to stress the fact that challenging Kevin Rudd for the leadership that night was her own personal decision.

Gillard felt she had done the best she could, but it wasn't enough. Outside Canberra, few people had known about Rudd's chaotic management style, and to many it looked as if she had knifed her leader so she could move into the Lodge with her boyfriend. It would have been close to impossible to explain what had happened without the disrespect to Kevin Rudd she was determined to avoid.

She did not dwell on that, however. She felt she had made the right decision, she knew why, and she had the support of most of her colleagues. She was preoccupied with what lay ahead. 'Moving forward', her widely derided choice of an election slogan, encapsulated this view. There was no time to focus on the past. Public perception of what had happened could be dealt with later; there was nothing much she could do about it, and there was work to be done. At first her personal poll ratings skyrocketed, which reassured some of the more nervous members of her party: the prime minister was sure this would not last, and she was right.

Almost her first act was to call an election for 21 August, less than three months after she assumed office. There is a widespread view that she would have done better to wait for a few more months, to let the public become used to the idea of Julia Gillard PM.

'People tell me that,' she said. 'But politics never gives you the opportunity to run the control test. A big dramatic event had happened and I did feel very keenly that the Australian public needed to get a say in that. And besides, the level of media hysteria at the time was never going to let us settle down.'

The election campaign lasted only five weeks: for many voters and for much of the media it seemed interminable. Gillard looked uneasy and wooden, apparently weighing every anodyne word she spoke, and operating, it seemed, from behind an expressionless mask. Some commentators later suggested that, because of the way she came to office, she had a Macbeth-like inner conflict in taking on the prime ministership, perhaps feeling that her accession, her authority, were not legitimate. She disagreed. 'Psychologically, no, I don't feel that, and I didn't feel that at the time,' she said. 'When I came to the office I was having internal battles to sort the whole show out. I put most of my energy into that, rather than the externals of presentation and so on.'

She was of course seriously hamstrung by a harsh political fact. During any election campaign, the incumbent government runs on its record. The ALP had done some impressive things, not least making sure Australia survived the global economic crisis. But Gillard could not take advantage of these reforms: having deposed the man who had been in charge, how could she justify using them for herself?

Not surprisingly a clear, compelling and assured narrative, which was what the electorate wanted and needed to hear, eluded her. At the same time Leader of the Opposition Tony Abbott was coming across as a likeable, knockabout bloke, delivering his slogans with ease and apparent sincerity. During the campaign Gillard made some odd, impulsive decisions – the announcement that she would present the 'real Julia', the citizens' assembly on climate change. Policy on the run, said her critics. Doesn't know what she's doing.

And then there were the leaks from Rudd supporters, later assumed to have been made with Rudd's knowledge or active support, and reported by senior press gallery journalist Laurie Oakes and others. It was said that Gillard had opposed the government's parental leave scheme as too expensive, that she had spoken out against the decision to raise the single-person age pension because 'elderly voters don't support us'. Most damaging of all was the report that Gillard had been instrumental in persuading Kevin Rudd to abandon his proposed emissions trading scheme because it was unpopular with the business interests Labor needed to have on side. Allied to the apparently half-hearted and piecemeal climate change policy she had brought to the election campaign, this story made many voters doubt that Gillard believed in climate change at all. It was a perception that was to have devastating effects on her prime ministership later.

The level of public engagement in the whole dismal and shabby campaign was summed up by journalist George Megalogenis: '[This is] a campaign without clarity, let alone conviction. It's what you get when a former journalist is pitted against a former lawyer.'[2] The timing of the one televised debate between Gillard and Abbott, on 25 July, was changed because it clashed with the finale of *MasterChef*.

The federal election result became clear early in September after a protracted period of uncertainty. Labor won exactly the same number of seats as the Liberal–National Party coalition – seventy-two each, though on raw numbers more people had actually voted for the Coalition.

The differences in the state votes were potentially troubling for future Commonwealth–State relations. According to ABC election analyst Antony Green,[3] Labor recorded its highest two-party-preferred result since World War II in Victoria and Tasmania, and second best in South Australia. It also had its worst two-party-preferred result in Western Australia since 1977, and in New South Wales all the gains of the

2007 federal election had been wiped out. And there was a huge swing against Labor in Queensland, Kevin Rudd's home state. Without the swing to Labor in the southern states, the Coalition would certainly have won government.

Gillard was faced with only the second hung federal parliament in Australian political history. In order to govern at all she would have to depend on a handful of crossbenchers, representing mainly conservative electorates.

And so, from the very beginning of her prime ministership, Julia Gillard apparently had everything against her. She had come to the office in a way that many people did not like or respect. She would be trying to govern against a resurgent and invigorated Opposition led by Tony Abbott, an implacably belligerent leader with a talent for crafting glib, simplistic and highly effective slogans, and whose party knew that all it needed to topple Labor was one scandal, one mistake, one seat changing hands. She faced dissension from within her own parliamentary party, not all of whose members had supported the ousting of Rudd. She would have to handle hostility from large sections of the mainstream media that would continue to back the Coalition: already some journalists were speculating openly and at length about her competence and political future. And she was standing before an electorate whose message to her was: 'Convince us.'

A different kind of woman might have been content to try and ingratiate herself with the public, be guided by the media and opinion polls, make soothing noises, do very little, enjoy the kudos of being Australia's first woman PM. To not stir up further resistance by trying to do difficult things. Do her best to stay out of trouble.

Julia Gillard was not that kind of woman.

Even before the election result had been made clear, Gillard knew she would have to depend on the votes of certain non-aligned crossbench MPs in the House of Representatives: New South Wales country independents and former National Party MPs Rob Oakeshott and Tony Windsor, Tasmanian independent Andrew Wilkie, and Greens MP Adam Bandt. On election night she made a point of contacting them, inviting them by telephone to meet and discuss areas of agreement and differences.

She had already made a deal with the Greens. In return for guarantees to help a re-elected Labor government to run its full term, Adam Bandt and Greens leader Bob Brown had asked for a range of policy undertakings, including a revised carbon pricing scheme. They also asked for government-supported dental care, a feasibility study on high-speed rail and a full parliamentary debate on Australia's involvement in the war in Afghanistan. The mining tax was not mentioned, nor was welfare policy or federal regulation of coal seam drilling, all issues the Greens brought up later.

Perhaps because he assumed that the Coalition had already won the election or would shortly do so, Tony Abbott did not contact the independents for several days. When he did, his tone was less than conciliatory. Tony Windsor, an MP during premier Nick Greiner's NSW hung parliament in the late 1980s and therefore knowledgeable about the kinds of deals resulting from uncertain electoral outcomes, said that Abbott probably assumed Oakeshott and Windsor would support the Coalition because they both represented conservative electorates.

In the end they both agreed to support the Gillard government, with Windsor quick to say that their agreement was with the PM, not necessarily the party she led – a position he maintained, and acted on, for the following three years. Both he and Oakeshott said that the government's planned $3.7 billion National Broadband Network, a scheme to deliver fast broadband to 93 per cent of Australian households, had been critical in ensuring their support because of its importance to Australians outside the cities. They were also very conscious of the need to guarantee parliamentary stability.

Throughout her term, Gillard made a point of holding weekly meetings with the independents during parliamentary sitting weeks, knowing that their support was critical to the survival of her government. By all accounts, there was a high level of respect and liking between her and the New South Wales independents. Tony Windsor commented that, 'She is warm, capable and always structured in discussions – there isn't an "anything will do" feel to it, more like working through things. I think the first thing that makes her good is that she doesn't blow her cool. I have never seen her ruffled, or even hurried, though she'd have to be, or to get angry and try to dud us.'[4]

Rob Oakeshoot spoke of Gillard's capacity to take drama out of emotional issues: 'She understands people have passion, that's why we're in politics, and those passions and constituents may not be the same as hers, but she can understand and work with that.'

Relationships with all crossbench MPs, however, have not always been distinguished by mutual admiration. This is certainly true of Gillard's interactions with the Greens. A number of people from within the ALP organisation were never comfortable about making an alliance with Bob Brown and his party, believing that the Greens, a one-issue party, would have too much influence on the government. There were potential threats to the arrangement in January 2012 when Brown accused Gillard of 'a breach of honour' in allowing logging in almost 2000 hectares of Tasmania's native forests. (The federal and Tasmanian governments, which had agreed on a deal to protect 430 000 hectares of Tasmanian forests in 2011, had decided to excise 1950 hectares because other areas of forest could not be logged in time to honour existing timber contracts.) However, he did not withdraw Greens support on the grounds that the Coalition's forests policy was even worse.

But in February 2013 Brown's successor, Christine Milne, announced that the Greens would no longer abide by its agreement with Labor. She cited disagreements over policy, specifically the mining tax but also the government's policies regarding asylum seekers. Milne fell short of withdrawing Greens support entirely, though, leading to some ponderous media jokes about divorce that does not include separation.

Tasmanian independent Andrew Wilkie also fell out with Gillard over policy, this time on gambling and poker machines. His reason for supporting her government had been her pledge to introduce mandatory pre-commitment technology on gaming machines by 2014.[5] Gillard later said there was insufficient support in Parliament for this, quoting a Productivity Commission recommendation that the new technology be trialled first. Early in 2012 Wilkie announced that he was tearing up his agreement because Gillard had broken her promise. The relationship between the two cooled appreciably after that, though Wilkie, while asserting his independence, continued broadly to support most of Gillard's government initiatives.

The media hailed these signs of rupture, big and small, as the beginning of the end for the government and for Gillard personally. But as it turned out the actions of two MPs – one from the ALP, the other from the Coalition – emerged as greater threats to Gillard's control and maintenance of power than a combative Opposition or disputes with independent MPs.

Craig Thomson came into Parliament in 2007 as ALP member for Dobell on the NSW Central Coast. He had previously been national secretary of the Health Services Union, from which he resigned when he became an MP. In 2008 the HSU alleged that he had made improper use of his union-issued corporate credit card, a charge Thomson denied. But more and more details came out about the corruption at the heart of the HSU that implicated Thomson, and in April 2012 Gillard, having previously declared her confidence in him, suspended him from the ALP, a decision he did not dispute.

The HSU was threatened with deregistration by the federal workplace relations tribunal, Fair Work Australia, which also instigated civil proceedings against Thomson. He was arrested and charged with fraud in February 2013 and declared his intention to contest all charges, which at the time of writing he was still facing. Had he been convicted and forced to resign from Parliament, the subsequent by-election could have been disastrous for Gillard's administration, given the fine balance of numbers between the ALP and the Coalition.

Equally tricky for Gillard's government was the concurrent case of Peter Slipper. MP for the Queensland seat of Fisher, Slipper had been a Liberal government whip in the late 1990s and parliamentary secretary to prime minister John Howard. In government and Opposition, he was also a member of several parliamentary committees. In 2010 it was alleged that he had misused his parliamentary travel entitlements, though he said he had been cleared.

In September 2010, following an agreement by Labor, the Greens and the Coalition that the deputy speaker of the House of Representatives would be drawn from the Opposition, Slipper was elected. Fourteen months later in November 2011 on the last sitting day of Parliament, the ALP's Harry Jenkins unexpectedly resigned as speaker, causing a frenzy of head counting in both major parties. Slipper was elected as speaker and chose to resign from the Liberal National Party, becoming an independent. His vote with the Gillard government would give the ALP another much-needed vote on the floor of the House.

Early the following year Slipper was under investigation by the Federal Police for misusing taxpayer-funded travel vouchers and – more sensationally – for allegations of sexual harassment brought against him by a member of his staff, James Ashby. The Coalition, a section of which were moving to disendorse Slipper in favour of former Liberal MP Mal Brough (who had lost his own seat in the 2007 election) demanded that Slipper resign as speaker. Gillard refused to countenance such an action until due legal process had been carried out.

In April 2012, however, Slipper decided to step aside anyway, and he was replaced by Labor MP Anna Burke. As for the accusations of sexual harassment, after a lot of unpleasant publicity for Slipper, including the publication of private correspondence between him and his accuser, the Federal Court threw out the case against him, with the judge making scathing comments about the way Slipper had been treated.

Every Australian parliament – every parliamentary body in the world – has always had its share of drones and timeservers. If the administration is sufficiently robust, these members are tolerated, worked around where necessary. But when the government is unpopular, or on a knife edge – as Gillard's was for almost its whole running time – the actions of the Slippers and the Thomsons are thrown into sharp relief, with much press comment about their conduct tarnishing the reputation of Australian democracy. It is to the credit of those who wanted to make Gillard's government function properly that these issues were not more disruptive than they were.

Indeed, according to Rob Oakeshott, under Gillard parliamentary procedures improved.[6] Committee structures worked better, with backbenchers given more opportunities to bring forward legislation. There was also a record number of private members' bills. In fact, over the life of the Gillard government the number of bills passed in the House of Representatives, including Senate-initiated and private members' bills, was nearly 600. Gillard government initiatives include the National Disability Insurance Scheme; the National Broadband Network; the increase in the superannuation guarantee from 9 to 12 per cent; increased spending on education, hospitals, mental health services and Australia's ageing population; an increase in means-tested pensions, allowances and family benefits, and the salaries of community service workers; plain packaging for cigarettes; paid parental leave; setting up a Royal Commission into Institutional Responses to Child Sexual Abuse; the raising of the tax-free threshold; and changes to the taxation of superannuation in favour of lower-income earners.

One way of looking at a successful government is its ability to pass legislation: at the very least this signals a PM who is good at getting things done. According to a blog published in *The Guardian* on 6 July, Julia Gillard has the highest rate of passing legislation of any prime minister in our history.[7] And this in a hung parliament, with hostility from large sections of the media and an Opposition baying for her blood.

Unfinished business

Julia Gillard was often criticised for being a nuts-and-bolts legislator, a fixer of problems, rather than a prime minister with a larger vision, an overriding narrative of Australian society and Australia's place in the world.

Gillard was never the kind of person, or politician, who constantly reverted to rhetoric or abstractions about nationhood: that kind of talk was alien to her thoroughly practical temperament. Her view of the prime ministership reflected this turn of mind. 'The biggest learning curve in being PM is learning how the various parts of government fit together,' she told me.[1] 'You really get better at working out what government is and what it can be; you stop understanding it in silos and programs and get much more of a sense of how it works as a whole.

'Before I became PM, I had experience with some very important silos in government – education, industrial relations, health and immigration and the work I did in the national security committee – but in this job you get to stand and survey and put it all together.

'Schoolkids always ask me, What's the best thing about being PM? They expect me to say, Well I've got this really cool plane (which I don't, Obama's got the really cool plane). But the best thing, really, is that you get to make decisions about what you think is going to make this a better nation. You get to discuss it, fashion it, put it together and implement it, and then you get to see it. You go to a school and a teacher tells you that a particular child is doing better because of some facility we've given them that they didn't have before.

'That's the best.'

You get very little discussion about lights on hills when you talk to Julia Gillard. In any case talk about vision in politics is usually the product of hindsight: government seen through a rear-view mirror, as it were. Julia Gillard's career – student political leader, then industrial lawyer, then MP and prime minister – is the story of a thoroughly pragmatic woman, a problem solver, someone who followed a plan or a brief and who would rather get things done than talk about them. But as Rob Oakeshott said, Gillard understands that politics can be a passionate business. Under her enviably calm and self-possessed exterior were certainly convictions that shaped her political life.

Gillard often outlined what drove her in politics and it came down to her belief that every Australian citizen should be given equal opportunity, first of all through a good education, to contribute to a productive society. She expressed this several years before she became PM – indeed, on the day she was sworn in as Kevin Rudd's deputy. She said: 'After . . . years of economic growth, too many individuals and communities remain caught in an intergenerational cycle of low educational attainment, high unemployment, poor health, high imprisonment rates and child abuse . . . [I]t's going to be my job to bring these people and these communities back within the economic and social mainstream. Simply put, productivity improvement can't be separated from the idea of fairness.'[2]

She expressed these views again in more detail when she gave the inaugural Gough Whitlam Oration in March 2011: 'We have moved beyond the days of big government and big welfare, to opportunity through education and inclusion through participation . . . fair access to opportunity has been our historic mission.

'We have always acknowledged that access to opportunity comes with obligations to seize that opportunity. To work hard, to set your alarm clocks early, to ensure your children are in school. We are the party of work, not welfare, that's why we respect the efforts of the brickie and look with a jaundiced eye at the lifestyle of the socialite. The Labor culture values effort more than status.'[3]

Gillard's words are consistent with a great deal of the legislation that her government put in place. And even in the fraught and difficult atmosphere caused by her accession to the leadership, she gave clear notice that she intended to carry out some of the policy initiatives that she and Kevin Rudd had set in train. The first of these was probably the biggest: putting a price on the carbon that Australian businesses and industries released into the atmosphere.

This was intended as a modified initiative of Kevin Rudd's – to set up an emissions trading scheme in response to the challenge of increasing Australia's prosperity in the face of climate change. The original idea was straightforward: industries that are heavy users of atmosphere-polluting greenhouse gases were to be allocated an emissions quota, and if they emitted less than this they could sell the difference to another industry that wanted to emit more.

In response to a review by leading economist

Professor Ross Garnaut, the Rudd government had recommended a 2020 target range for greenhouse gas emissions of between 5 and 15 per cent less than 2000 levels, though they ignored Garnaut's advice that industry compensation should be kept to a minimum. The proposed scheme satisfied nobody. The conservation movement accused the government of caving in to the big polluters, while various industries, especially mining, declared that Australian companies were being shackled with an unjustifiable burden.

The Greens rejected the proposal in Parliament on the grounds that it was weak, but then Opposition leader Malcolm Turnbull, who as minister for the environment in the Howard government had proposed something similar, committed the Coalition to supporting the proposed bill. The conservatives in his party were outraged and shortly afterwards Turnbull lost the leadership. His successor, Tony Abbott, wasted little time in declaring climate change to be 'crap', and the bill was rejected.

That, plus the dismal failure of the Copenhagen Climate Change Conference in setting legally binding targets for the countries of the world to reduce carbon pollution, effectively cancelled the introduction of the ETS. But the result could not be simply shrugged off as a win-some, lose-some initiative because Rudd had said that climate change was the most important moral issue of our time and had made the Copenhagen summit into a personal crusade.

The bill, twice rejected, could have become the trigger for a double dissolution of parliament, and some of Rudd's colleagues urged him to go for that. They argued that according to the polls most Australians wanted something done about climate change, and Rudd would be nailing his environmental colours to the mast. It was high-wire politics, but the odds looked good. Just before Christmas 2009 Rudd met with Wayne Swan, Julia Gillard, minister for employment participation Mark Arbib and senior staff to discuss this. However, they talked him out of going to the people on the issue because they said it was too risky.

At the same time, the ALP shelved a multi-million-dollar campaign to advertise the ETS – regarded as an indispensable part of getting the electorate used to major reform – because it would not pass the approval processes that Rudd had set up in 2007 as part of his promise to end expensive political advertising. Arbib and ALP federal secretary Karl Bitar were soon urging him to get rid of the ETS altogether.

When the Senate defeated the government's carbon pollution reduction bill for the third time in February 2010, it looked as if the whole thing was dead in the water. Rudd postponed introducing the trading scheme for a further three years. Many Australians concluded that Kevin Rudd and his government had squibbed the climate change issue completely, and Rudd's poll numbers began to slide.

On 27 September, three weeks after the 2010 election result had been declared, Julia Gillard announced plans for a multi-party committee that would build consensus on tackling climate change. It was set up to have two representatives from the Coalition, two from the Greens and representation from independents and experts on the issue, including Professor Garnaut. The Coalition refused the government's invitation, with environment spokesman Greg Hunt saying that membership of the committee meant agreeing that climate change was real, which was 'undemocratic'.

On 24 February 2011 the committee announced its decision: a carbon pricing scheme would be put in place on 1 July 2012. This would have a simple premise. As Gillard explained the scheme in Parliament on 1 March: 'We will put a price on . . . every unit of carbon pollution. It will be paid for by businesses and as a result, because our business community is smart and adaptable and innovative, they will work out ways of pursuing their business and generating less carbon pollution.'

The scheme was set up to cover a range of large business and industrial facilities that produced about 60 per cent of Australia's pollutant carbon, including from electricity generation, stationary energy, landfills, wastewater, the transport sector and industrial processes. It did not cover agriculture, most Australian businesses or households. The aim was that by 2050 emissions would be reduced by 80 per cent of 2000 levels. Compensation, at a level to be determined later, would be available to out-of-pocket households and certain businesses.

Carbon-producing businesses would be required to give annual reports about their emissions or potential emissions, with the obligation to surrender one carbon unit for every tonne of carbon dioxide or equivalent that they had produced in that year. In the first three years of the scheme, the price of carbon units would be fixed and emissions unlimited. After 2015 the carbon price would be set by the market, based on the advice of the newly set up Climate Change Authority, which would work with the Productivity Commission. The annual cap would decrease as Australia's emissions reduction targets increased, and the number of carbon units issued each year would equal the amount capped by the scheme. After three years of this flexible price period, the role of the price cap would be reviewed.

The scheme was ridiculed almost immediately, with objections led by Abbott's Opposition and its allies in business and the media. They referenced the election-campaign leak that stated Gillard had tried to talk Rudd out of his proposed emissions trading scheme and her assertion on 16 August 2010 that 'there will be no carbon tax under the government I lead'.

Julia Gillard has denied she counselled Rudd against a scheme to tackle climate change. She said, 'We were elected in 2007 to do an emissions trading scheme, which I certainly wanted. Penny Wong went to hell and back about it, and it got rejected. Turnbull wanted it and then the Liberal Party changed, then Copenhagen happened and that disappointed the world and us, and the chaotic images from the conference undermined the community attitude and wish for a climate change policy.

'Australia was in drought, there was great focus on the weather and a sense that action was needed, but as the drought broke – and the drought was synonymous with climate change to many people – so the sense of urgency disappeared. And then the GFC happened, which meant people had to think about other issues.

'Climate change sceptics had put their acid drip on, and were undermining public belief, and of course the images that came out of Copenhagen didn't help. Against that backdrop, my view was that we should get in and fight for it, and if we didn't we'd have to work out what to say to the Australian people: we couldn't deal with this half-heartedly. And we had a set of internal discussions, and then we decided what was going in the Budget, and all of that leaked in a way that didn't enable any of us, including Kevin, to properly explain the issues and decisions.'[4] The Rudd scheme did not mention the accounting issues, the costs and compensation involved: many people's sticking points.

As the trained lawyer she was, Gillard continued to broadcast the facts about her new carbon pricing scheme, presumably believing that logic and reason would triumph over doubt and mistrust. But accusations that she had lied to the electorate refused to go away – fuelled no doubt by the continuing disquiet about her accession to office in the first place.

She appeared unwilling to acknowledge the effect this particular barrage of negativity might have on voters who needed to handle a whole new – and counterintuitive – set of policy formulations. Australians were being asked to make sacrifices now, to compromise their way of life, to compromise progress, all for a greater good that was invisible.

Instead, Gillard tried to switch the focus to

Abbott's negativity about climate change, which only served to spotlight the Opposition and therefore give the Coalition and the denialists more traction on the issue. 'The tax will be permanent, the compensation will be temporary, and that's why so many Australian families quite understandably realise that this is a giant con job from a government which lied to them before the last election,' declared Abbott. Gillard and her climate change minister, Greg Combet, implicitly accepted the Coalition's terminology that this was a 'carbon tax', instead of pointing out that the government was asking companies to pay for the pollution they caused. It was a classic example – among the first of many – of the government's inability to gain traction against the simplistic sloganeering of the Opposition.

Gillard's view that negative opinion was less important than getting on with the job was not of service to her here. She would have done better to tell the electorate the truth as soon as the criticism surfaced: that she had never sought to mislead the public over this issue. Faced with an election result that nobody could have anticipated and knowing that she needed the support of the Greens in order to stay in office, Gillard had crafted a policy that more or less satisfied them and achieved the result she wanted.

It is difficult to know how she could have spoken frankly on this without sounding apologetic – anathema to her and hardly justified – but she could perhaps have adopted the words of economist John Maynard Keynes. When accused of changing his position on monetary policy during the Depression, Keynes had retorted, 'When my information changes, I alter my conclusions. What do you do, sir?'

Ignoring Abbott's implacability and his populist success, and trusting that if the bills became law the whole argument would subside, Julia Gillard proceeded to do what she did best: negotiate. For months she and Greg Combet spoke to stakeholders inside and outside Parliament, explaining the new bills' implications for the business community and ways to invest in renewable energy sources.

On 7 November 2011, the eighteen clean energy bills passed through the House of Representatives, carried by 74 votes to 72, and the Senate (36 to 32). Through sheer determination and negotiating power Julia Gillard had achieved something that had defeated John Howard, Brendan Nelson, Malcolm Turnbull and Kevin Rudd – and she had done it from minority government.

With the Opposition already ahead in the polls, Abbott lost no time in declaring his intention to repeal the legislation the moment the Coalition came to office. Shadow Treasurer Joe Hockey warned companies that a future Coalition government would also seek to reverse funding commitments to renewable energy projects under the $10 billion Clean Energy Finance Corporation, which it would scrap.

When the Carbon Pollution Reduction Scheme came into effect in July 2012, the sky did not fall in. Household electricity and gas bills did go up by about 9 per cent as predicted; Treasury's estimates that the carbon pricing scheme would add just 0.7 per cent to the CPI also came to pass.

At the time of writing, evidence suggests that the CPRS has been accepted by business, and that it is beginning to have the desired effect on emission reduction. The Coalition's intention to scrap the 'great big new tax' has been met with less wholehearted endorsement than they might have wished. Abolishing the CPRS would mean reversing all the tax cuts funded by the carbon revenue, and some electricity suppliers have warned that power prices would increase because plans for billions of dollars of new infrastructure would be compromised. Funding commitments to renewable energy projects would also be reversed, which has caused some unease in the business community. It is sometimes forgotten that the industries for which carbon pricing is important, including steel, aluminium and oil refining, will probably end up paying less than 10 per cent of the actual carbon price because of the free permits arrangement. The CPRS is not a crippling impost for industry, let alone the 'wrecking ball' that Abbott asserted would be driven through the Australian economy.

But the fate of the carbon pricing legislation remains to be seen, and not just because of the Coalition's opposition to it. At the end of April, the European Parliament proposed postponing the sale of 900 million carbon emission allowances for several years. This has severe implications for the Australian government's bottom line, for the revenue from the pricing of carbon will be lower than budgeted for. This is still a problem for the Opposition, should they win government and abolish the carbon pricing mechanism, because even with diminished revenue they are still locked into the same tax cuts and benefits increases. So they would have to find more money to pay polluters to reduce their emissions – and the Opposition's direct action policy is reliant on the Budget for funding.

Another tranche of Rudd's unfinished government business was the Resource Super Profits Tax.

Intended to ensure that Australian taxpayers were compensated by the largely foreign-owned mining companies exploiting the country's mineral resources, this was a proposed 40 per cent tax on the proportion of the profits above the ten-year Commonwealth Government bond rate made by mining and petroleum companies from minerals mined or quarried, including sand, gold, nickel and uranium. This tax would be payable on the realised value of resource deposits, and onshore and oil projects would be subject to it. States and territories would be able to keep existing royalties, but the federal government would give companies a refundable credit for state royalties currently paid. The money raised from the RSPT would be used to increase the superannuation guarantee rate from 9 per cent to 12 per cent.

Critics of the scheme – and there were many – declared that the RSPT cut in at an absurdly low level, that it should be applied only to new projects so that prospective investors could take the new tax into account, and that it should differentiate between particular mineral resources.[5] Moreover, because treasurer Wayne Swan had declared that if a mining investment project incurred un-deducted costs the government would refund owners a proportion of the loss, the taxpayer would be liable.

The RSPT was widely considered another example of policymaking on the run. There was also resentment about it within Cabinet: resources minister Martin Ferguson had been told the details only a few days before they were made public.

The mining industry mounted a $22 million advertising campaign against the proposals, and anti-mining tax ads were also a strong feature of the 2010 election campaign. These were countered by the government and abandoned by mutual agreement when Gillard was confirmed as prime minister.

Gillard moved swiftly to introduce a replacement for the RSPT in consultation with some of Australia's largest mining companies, and announced the result in July 2010. The new impost was called the Minerals Resource Rent Tax, and it extended the existing petroleum resource rent tax to all onshore oil and gas projects, including coal seam gas. However, the new tax, at a rate of 30 per cent, would be applied to the value of the resource itself, rather than that added by the miner. Mining projects would attract a 25 per cent extraction allowance that would reduce taxable profits, with the allowance proposed to be set at the long-term government bond rate plus 7 per cent. State royalties would be deductible, and MRRT payments could also be deducted from company tax. Money raised from the tax would be used to fund a variety of government initiatives, including family allowances and tax relief for small business. Early estimates were that the tax would ultimately raise about $13.4 billion annually.

Mining companies were loud in their outrage, declaring that the new tax would fatally impede growth of the mining sector. They were aided by the Opposition, with Tony Abbott predicting that towns that depend on mining, such as Whyalla in South Australia, would disappear. On the other hand, those who thought the mining companies had got off lightly for years thought the government had not gone far enough, that the tax was inadequate and would fail to achieve the desired result.

It was subsequently discovered that the tax agreement signed by Julia Gillard, treasurer Wayne Swan and resources minister Martin Ferguson and the heads of Australia's three big mining companies, BHP Billiton, Rio Tinto and Xstrata, contained a serious drafting error, allowing the mining companies to increase their deductions if low profits meant they owed less resource tax than their royalty payments.

The Mining Resources Rent Tax raised a great deal less than originally anticipated. Instead of the $2 billion Wayne Swan had estimated for the 2012–13 financial year, it brought in just over $100 million.

To a Senate committee in April 2013 Professor Ross Garnaut said that the tax was so flawed that in its current form it might never raise any significant revenue. He blamed the structure of the agreement, in particular the clauses on state government mineral royalties, and the advantage taken by larger established companies, who lowered their exposure to the tax by citing the market value of existing mines. He added that though transitional arrangements for past expenditure were complex in terms of what constituted profitable projects, the way the government had chosen to operate was extremely generous to established projects.

Though the MRRT did not achieve its purpose, it had very little adverse effect, if any, on mining sector investment, contrary to the predictions of doom. Indeed, investment in Australia's mining sector grew strongly, from $47 billion in 2010–11 to an expected $119 billion in 2012–13, though at the time of writing this appeared to be slowing down. In April 2013 a leading independent US-based mining analyst declared Australia the safest place for mining investment in the world, ahead of Canada and Chile – a result that was consistent with that of the previous three years.[6] Given the global signs of caution about mining investment this may mean less than it once might have.

The point is that a mining profits tax was needed, and the MRRT has certainly not destroyed Australia's mining industry. But it is surprising that a tax that has produced so much antagonism towards the Rudd and Gillard governments has done so little to spread benefits of the mining industry among the wider population – that the Rudd and Gillard governments gave themselves so much trouble for so little result.

Two steps forward, one step back

> 'But if we just said let's share money out, let's keep the current system and put money on top of it, then every inequity, every disparity, everything wrong with the current system would be taken with us into the future.'
> *Julia Gillard talking about her education reforms,* AM, *ABC Radio, 15 April 2013*

For Julia Gillard, equality of opportunity and equality of education are inseparable. Almost from the moment she came to prominence in federal politics she emphasised this, pointing out how important education had been in her own life and asserting that access to a good education should be the birthright of every Australian child. It really was her signature policy, her political leitmotif. It guided her oversight of the 2009 Building the Education Revolution program, the $16 billion economic stimulus package that, by building new facilities or refurbishing existing ones for primary and secondary schools Australia-wide, was an important element in the infrastructure spending that helped Australia dodge the bullet of the global economic crisis.

At the time the program was heavily criticised for being profligate, and critics declared it would not provide any jobs in the building sector until after the economy recovered. In fact – as three independent reviews of the scheme found – the BER created jobs as well as schools infrastructure. As a stimulus package it was highly successful, as its beneficiaries widely acknowledged: 10000-odd school projects were undertaken Australia-wide, with complaints from fewer than 300 schools.

Gillard's other wideranging change to Australia's educational structure – the national curriculum and the 2008 NAPLAN (National Assessment Program – Literacy and Numeracy), which set benchmarks for students in years 3, 5, 7 and 9 all over Australia and was supplemented by the MySchool website in early 2010 – brought questions about inequality of educational opportunity into stark relief. One cause for this was inequality of funding for schools in the different educational sectors.

Extending public funding to private schools has always been a difficult issue for Labor governments. Since private schools first got funding from the federal government, in 1963 when Menzies guaranteed funding for science laboratories in schools throughout the country, Labor has never cared to reverse such a popular trend. Gough Whitlam, Bob Hawke and Mark Latham all learned that 'don't cut government funding for rich private schools' is the education policy equivalent of 'don't start a land war in Asia'. What makes the whole funding question even more difficult for any federal government is that each of the six states and two territories has separate sectors of government and private schools, with their own funding mix from different sources.

Gillard, however, tackled the inequality question head on. In 2010 she commissioned a Review of Funding for Schooling to develop a funding system for Australian schools that would be transparent, fair, financially sustainable and effective. The review panel, chaired by businessman and philanthropist David Gonski, spent a year evaluating Commonwealth, state and territory schools funding, and examining the needs of students from schools across the government, Catholic and independent schools sectors. In November 2011 they presented their final report, which the government released, along with its initial response, in February 2012.

The basic message of the Gonski Report was more straightforward and starker than many had expected: the quality of Australian education was declining. The report stated that in 2000 Australia had been second in the OECD countries in reading and scientific literacy, and third in mathematical literacy. Nine years later, six countries outperformed Australia in reading and scientific literacy, and twelve in mathematics. There was a significant gap, too, between the country's highest- and lowest-performing students, with the latter failing to meet minimum NAPLAN standards of achievement. Students from disadvantaged socioeconomic and Indigenous backgrounds tended to be at the bottom of the heap. And at all levels of government – federal, state and local – funding arrangements were unnecessarily complex and wasteful.

The Gonski Report recommended that funding should be increased by about $6.5 billion a year across all primary and secondary schooling sectors, with the greater part going to the government sector because it had more students, including disadvantaged ones. NAPLAN scores would continue to be used as the benchmark for schools performance, and the socioeconomic status of schools would also be considered. One-third of this money would come from the Commonwealth, with the rest negotiable across all levels of government. In the case of non-government schools, Gonski recommended that public funding be adjusted according to the capacity of parents and the school community to contribute. The scheme would be administered by a new organisation called the National Schools Resourcing Body.

The Gonski Report attracted the same kind of criticism from educational and state-funding bodies as had the Gillard NAPLAN changes: that it depended too heavily on a one-size-fits-all model without taking account of variations between the states or schools within the states, and that different states' educational strengths and weaknesses were not being sufficiently acknowledged.

Gonski also had two big stumbling blocks. For the reforms to succeed, there had to be willing cooperation between the states and the Commonwealth. This was always going to be a problem for the Gillard government, since the most populous states in the country had Liberal–National Party governments. Further, in trying to get the Gonski reforms through, Gillard could not say exactly where the money was coming from. Gonski's $6.5 billion per year was on top of an annual state and federal schools budget of around $40 billion: the Mining Resources Rent Tax, which had been earmarked for the Gonski program among others, had raised much less than expected. The government would have to make cuts to other Commonwealth programs to pay for it.

State premiers were not slow to come forward with their own objections, illustrating one of the enduring features of state–federal relations in Australia: the resentment-fuelled opposition of state administrations to anything that looks even remotely like centralised control, especially concerning traditional state responsibilities. Then Victorian premier Ted Baillieu rejected the plan on the grounds that the states had no say in what would be cut and what not, and that accountability for spending would be removed from the schools' governing bodies, parents and local communities, and handed to distant bureaucrats in Canberra. He also proposed that disadvantaged students should be funded individually. His stand was supported by Queensland premier Campbell Newman and Western Australia's Colin Barnett.

Nothing more happened for a while. Then, on the weekend of 13 and 14 April 2013, Julia Gillard abruptly announced a series of initiatives set out in the Gonski plan. Commonwealth funding for schools would be calculated according to a new Schooling Resource Standard: there would be a base amount for every primary and secondary school student, with loadings for schools according to specific student needs, especially in the areas of disability, Indigenous education, limited English skills, location and class size. The base amounts would be $9271 per primary student and $12 193 for every secondary student. The cost of implementing the reforms would be $14.1 billion over six years – much less than Gonski had originally asked for.

Funding some of the shortfall would be $2.3 billion previously intended for the higher education sector. This caused an outcry among students and workers in tertiary education. Gillard and her minister Craig Emerson were quick to point out that spending on universities would not be cut, the rate of funding increase would just be slower, and the number of university places would not be decreased – Gillard even provided a graph on Twitter to prove it – but the damage had been done. Many echoed the words of Jeannie Rea, president of the National Tertiary Education Union, who said, 'The idea of cutting higher education to fund massive reforms in schooling, when the purpose of schooling is to prepare students for work and university, is ironic to say the least.'[1]

Almost without exception university vice-chancellors lined up to condemn the diminished university funding, painting bleak pictures of the impact on their universities. (However, one brave academic,

Dr Chandra Shah from Monash University, said the scale and impact of the cutbacks on tertiary institutions had been overstated.[2]) David Gonski himself, chancellor of the University of New South Wales, was not happy either, adding that the review panel had not been asked to consider how their final recommendations should be funded.

As far as public perception was concerned, cutting one part of the education sector to fund another seemed a crazy decision, and one that tarnished Gillard's legacy of education reform. Many stakeholders also felt that she had announced the Gonski reforms abruptly and without sufficiently wide consultation. For some mysterious reason, the government made little obvious attempt to counter criticism from interested parties, and gave no explanation as to why university funding had been targeted instead of other possible government programs and initiatives.

The Gonski initiatives gave the conservative state governments something of a problem. It was Paul Keating who said that nobody should ever get between a premier and a bag of money, and the new funding had substantial financial advantages. A large number of schools in Queensland, New South Wales and Victoria were heavily underfunded, but to accept Gillard's offer would lose the governments in those states political points. Gillard gave the premiers until

30 June to decide whether to sign up.

Western Australia, which funded its schools more generously than the other states because of its mining wealth and relatively small population, stood to get correspondingly less Commonwealth money and was loud in condemnation, with premier Colin Barnett denouncing Gonski as a terrible deal for his state. Others cried poor or said they might consider the scheme. And the federal Opposition, in the person of shadow education minister Christopher Pyne, quickly announced that unless the government could get a binding agreement from all states and territories, any future Abbott government would reject the reforms altogether. However, the independents in the House of Representatives signalled their agreement to the package, saying they could live with a slower rate of university funding if this meant improving primary and secondary schools.

Then on 23 April Barry O'Farrell, premier of New South Wales, caught the media – and probably the federal government – by surprise when he became the first state leader to sign up to the Gonski deal. This was widely hailed as an astute move, with the leader of Australia's most populous state signalling his reluctance to follow the federal Opposition line in everything, as well as enabling him to solve the problem of the electorally unpopular cuts he had made to education spending. O'Farrell's acquiescence caused a problem for Gillard, though: she could no longer say that all conservative state governments were opposed to giving the nation's children a first-class education, a strategic point that could have played well in the forthcoming election campaign. However, Gillard, who tended to regard successful policy outcomes as more significant than mere political advantage, seemed relieved and delighted.

The whole Gonski education reform project, though admirable in scope and boldly innovative, has left something to be desired in terms of execution. The amount of money allocated is far short of Gonski's recommendations, and the fraction of the funding going into loadings for disadvantaged schools was less than anticipated, and spread more thinly than Gonski asked for. The Gonski plan does not tackle the ways in which the $40 billion currently spent on schools each year could be better directed: the states are responsible for allocating most of this, and agreements between state-based school systems and teacher organisations are very specific about how schools will spend their resources.

Education policy will likely continue to be a policy battleground for some time yet.

When Kevin Rudd was prime minister, he made a personal crusade out of hospital reform. The plan he announced early in 2010 was that the Commonwealth would gradually take control of hospital funding, and that primary health care would become solely a federal responsibility. To pay for this, the states would give up 30 per cent of their GST revenue, which would be diverted directly to hospitals. But at the time it was by no means certain that the Commonwealth had the power to do what Rudd proposed, and the states resented what they saw as Rudd's high-handed take-it-or-leave-it approach. In the end the plan was rejected.

Soon after coming to office Gillard sought to revamp the Rudd health reform plan. After a great deal of negotiation including a fifteen-month stand-off with the Western Australian government, she and health minister Tanya Plibersek managed to get all the heads of government to work in partnership on a national health policy.

The agreement signed at the Council of Australian Governments meeting on 13 February 2011 introduced new state–Commonwealth financial arrangements for cost-sharing in the public hospital system, and a mutual agreement to plan for GP and primary health services, as well as further reforms in mental and dental health and aged care. The

Commonwealth government would be responsible for establishing Medicare Locals and GP super clinics, upgrading and increasing community medical services, funding home and community care for the aged, and spending on training doctors and other health care professionals.

The Commonwealth would increase its contribution to hospital funding to be at least $16.4 billion between 2014 and 2020. State and territory governments would remain the managers of their own public hospital systems. And to compensate for their extra responsibilities, states and territories would be able to keep the 30 per cent of the GST revenue that had been earmarked for the Commonwealth under the Rudd plan. The states, however, had stringent reporting requirements. Gillard and Plibersek hailed this agreement as the most fundamental change to health care in Australia since Medicare.

However, two years later in March 2013, the deal was threatening to unravel. New national population data showed that Victorian state hospitals were not meeting their performance goals and in a strongly worded letter Gillard announced that she would send the money directly to local hospitals, bypassing the state government. The Queensland state government then said they planned to privatise parts of the hospital system, leaving Gillard and Plibersek less than impressed and threatening to take money from other Commonwealth funding allocations.

At the time of writing, this issue was unresolved.

Another difficult area, and one that Julia Gillard flagged as a priority from the beginning of her prime ministership, was that of asylum seeker policy. Immigration is another tricky issue for the ALP, which has a history of using compassionate language alongside labour market protectionism, with racism and xenophobia thrown in. It is not always convenient to remember that the labour movement enthusiastically supported the White Australia policy for a long time.

But at the end of World War II Australia needed immigrants for nation building, something recognised by both sides of politics. Immigration became a bipartisan issue: in the 1970s, for example, Liberal PM Malcolm Fraser was able to increase the numbers of Vietnamese refugees to Australia with the cooperation and support of the Labor Opposition. However under John Howard, bipartisanship went by the board, especially with regard to asylum seekers, whose treatment Howard astutely used as an issue to wedge the ALP. Howard's tough stance, expressed in his declaration that 'we will decide who comes to this country and the circumstances under which they come', was approved by many voters. Now Labor was caught between the Scylla of those in critical Labor seats with no sympathy for asylum seekers and the Charybdis of Labor supporters who wanted less harsh treatment for them.

In 2002, in Opposition under the leadership of Simon Crean, Gillard carefully crafted a response to the asylum seeker policy of John Howard's Coalition government. Gillard's policy asserted that under a Labor government 'border protection' would come first, there would be crackdowns on illegal workers, people smugglers would be severely punished, and mandatory detention would continue for asylum seekers while their applications for asylum were being processed. It could have been written by any Coalition political leader (except Malcolm Fraser), but was generally accepted by the ALP as a skilful and acceptable response to an extremely thorny issue. It confirmed Julia Gillard as a rising political star.

When Gillard came to office as prime minister, she made her view clear. Rejecting her predecessor Kevin Rudd's expressed desire for a 'big Australia', she said immigration had to be sustainable, and she also declared her support for the popular view that there should be 'strong management of our borders' (even though Australia is an island) and that asylum seekers should have their claims evaluated offshore. Perhaps she was trying to make up for having rushed out the ill-judged 'East Timor solution' just before the 2010 election, an initiative that failed after protests from the government of East Timor, who said they had not been properly consulted first.

Gillard's position on asylum seekers remained conservative. In May 2011 she and her minister for immigration Chris Bowen announced a bilateral agreement between Australia and Malaysia to trade asylum seekers. Under its terms 800 would-be arrivals by boat in Australia would be taken to Malaysia and in return Australia would take 4000 other refugees from Malaysia over four years. Gillard and Bowen denied that this was a new version of the Howard government's 2001 so-called Pacific solution – the policy that, to prevent boat people being assessed for refugee status on Australian soil, excised thousands of territorial islands from Australia's migration zone, opening the way for asylum seekers to be transported to detention camps on small Pacific island nations. No, said Gillard, this was part of a regional scheme for dealing with asylum seekers.

At first the agreement was hailed as a useful solution to the problem. But its great weakness, and indeed a weakness of the government's regional focus, was that so many countries in Australia's vicinity have bad human rights records. Critics of the government's plan, including the Greens, pointed out that asylum seekers would certainly be worse off by going to Malaysia than by being assessed in Australia.

The whole issue ended up in the High Court. On 31 August 2011 the court ruled that according to the Migration Act the minister could only send potential arrivals to a country with an effective legal system and one that would protect them while their cases were being assessed: Malaysia and its laws could not guarantee these terms. The High Court also doubted Malaysia's ability to meet the human rights standards laid down by the office of the United Nations High Commissioner for Refugees. By rejecting the Gillard policy, the High Court vindicated many voters' opposition to Gillard's perceived hard-heartedness.

In June 2012 Gillard invited an 'expert panel on asylum seekers' led by Air Chief Marshal Angus Houston, the retired chief of Australia's defence force, to report on ways to prevent asylum seekers from risking their lives on dangerous boat journeys to Australia, and to assess the source, transit and destination aspects of irregular migration. The terms of reference strongly hinted that offshore assessment would be desirable.

The report pointed out that in global terms Australia's alleged refugee problem scarcely rated: the country's geographical position meant that it had received only 2.5 per cent of the world's asylum seekers, and in contradiction of Tony Abbott's mantra of 'stop the boats', most of those came by air. Among the twenty-two recommendations that proposed an integrated solution was an affirmation of offshore assessment: that Nauru, Manus Island off Papua New Guinea and, with some important modifications, Malaysia would be suitable transit countries for asylum seekers.

The report also recommended that those seeking asylum in Australia would stay in the transit area for the same period of time that it would have taken them to get to Australia had their applications been assessed elsewhere: in other words, being sent to Nauru would confer no advantage. So the report endorsed Gillard's regional approach and urged negotiation and agreement with Malaysia in the future. It also recommended that Australia should significantly increase its humanitarian intake to 27000 per year within five years.

On ABC-TV's *Lateline* early in April 2013, panel member and refugee advocate Paris Aristotle emphasised that setting up a regional system to assess asylum seekers' claims was vital, and that proper safeguards should be put in place in detention centres.[3] These safeguards should include compliance with international standards on human rights, no arbitrary detention, and the provision of case management services and mental health programs. Aristotle emphasised that often arrangements with foreign governments, including those with Papua New Guinea, were not ideal and would take time to resolve. In May Gillard visited PNG and arranged for detention centres at Manus Island to be significantly upgraded.

Most of the Houston review recommendations have either been carried out or are in progress. Australia's humanitarian intake increased from 13750 to 20000 within the 2012–13 financial year, with refugees from Burma, Afghanistan, Iran and Malaysia, as well as Iraqi refugees from Syria, Turkey, Jordan and Lebanon.

On 15 May 2013 the federal government combined with the Opposition to pass an amendment to the Migration Act. Recommended by the Houston review, this was intended to deal with the cases in which asylum seekers arrive on the Australian mainland, bypassing the islands that the Howard government had excised from the migration zone. In keeping with the Houston review panel's expressed concern that 'all possible measures should be taken to avoid creating an incentive for people to take even greater risks with their lives by seeking to bypass excised offshore places to reach the Australian mainland', the bill recommended that asylum seekers who arrived anywhere in Australia would be given the same status as 'those who arrived at an excised offshore place', meaning they would be subject to mandatory detention in a designated place – Manus Island or Nauru – and could not apply for a visa without the decision of the minister.

The Greens and some independent MPs described this effective excision of Australia from the migration zone as 'a stain on our national character'. The Gillard government hoped that, in extending the regional system, the amendment would serve to make the question of asylum seekers less controversial and inflammatory, possibly to neutralise it as a 'wedge' issue.

Not long before she was deposed as prime minister, Gillard scheduled a meeting with the president of Indonesia, Susilo Bambang Yudhoyono, to discuss the government's regional approach in dealing with asylum seekers: Kevin Rudd went in her stead. It was already apparent that the Indonesian government were not in favour of the Coalition's asylum seeker policy – expressed in the phrase 'turn back the boats' – and Rudd poured further scorn on the idea. On Friday 5 July President Yudhoyono corroborated the view that the issue was regionally based. He announced a meeting of ministers from all affected countries to reach a cooperative and jointly responsible solution about people smuggling, border security and unauthorised boat arrivals. He said it was important to include representatives not only of transit and destination countries but also of countries of origin, including Afghanistan, Burma and Iran. He stressed that cooperation needed to be sincere and should involve all countries in the region.

Getting the message across

One bit of TV footage from Parliament said it all. On 14 June 2013, Julia Gillard, her voice choked with emotion, announced the passage of the National Disability Insurance Scheme bill. This was a landmark piece of legislation that was close to her heart: she had fought long and hard to get it through. The announcement of its success should have been a moment of triumph for her. But in the House of Representatives she faced a huge and empty expanse of green leather. Hardly anyone from the Opposition had bothered to turn up, even though the bill had received their support. And the reporting of the bill concentrated on 'Julia's tears', not the quality of the legislation or what it would mean for thousands of Australians, their carers and families.

It was yet another illustration of something that

had become abundantly clear from the moment of Gillard's accession to the prime ministership and the election that followed. With the support of the country independents, Labor had passed the only test needed to form government: a majority on the floor of the House of Representatives. But for the Opposition party deprived of victory by such a narrow margin, and for their supporters in the media and elsewhere, this constitutional fact was unlikely to be respected.

A Labor government is always going to have a rougher ride from most of the media than the other side of politics, mostly because media ownership in this country is largely concentrated in the hands of conservatives. Between them, Fairfax Media and Rupert Murdoch's News Corp Australia own eleven out of the twelve Australian capital city daily newspapers. News Corp Australia also owns magazines, suburban newspapers and regional and rural newspapers in every state of Australia, as well as the national broadsheet and the country's most influential 24-hour commercial TV channel.

Murdoch-owned media outlets criticised the Rudd government's stimulatory public spending during the global financial crisis, labelled the education revolution an unmitigated disaster, backed the mining companies during discussions of the mining resource rent tax and persistently criticised any attempt at pricing carbon. Gillard's accession to the prime ministership was treated with scorn. When John Hartigan was News Ltd's chief executive, he told ABC-TV's Leigh Sales that 'we have things we think as a company and individually as editors that need to be done. One of them is a leadership vacuum by minority government.'[1]

Climate change scepticism has been a consistent thread throughout Murdoch newspapers and other outlets, inhibiting widespread discussion of the issue. Dr Michael Coughlan, chief climatologist at the Bureau of Meteorology, said he gave up talking to *The Australian* because 'no matter how many times the scientific community refutes these arguments, they persist in putting them out, to the point where we believe there's little to be gained in the use of our time in responding.'[2]

Given the barrage of negative press Julia Gillard received over the three years of her prime ministership, the lack of discussion about the Coalition's policies and the hostility towards the Greens, her restraint in discussing the media – especially the Murdoch press — verged on the heroic. For a prime minister to trash the media, a vital part of getting her message across, would hardly have been a smart move, of course. And in any case, Gillard has always appeared astonishingly free of self-pity or excuse-making: the role of victim is not a congenial one for her.

'I'm not a conspiracy theorist,' she told me, 'and I don't judge every Murdoch paper as though it's the same entity. But some newspapers have certainly taken a view about us and our policies and haven't even tried to be objective and even-handed.

'I can pick up a newspaper, and there's a story on the front page about the government that is factually untrue, and it is never corrected. I think that genuinely this is something people should be worried about – obviously I have a view about it, but I think Australians should all be concerned.' All she said publicly to journalists about the treatment she and her government received was her comment when at the National Press Club she was asked to suggest ways in which journalists could lift their game. She said succinctly: 'Don't write crap. Can't be that hard. And when you have written complete crap, then I think you should correct it.'[3]

Gillard herself was sufficiently annoyed by 'crap' to threaten legal action against Murdoch's *Australian* in August 2011. The columnist Glenn Milne stated that while working for law firm Slater & Gordon she had lived with her then partner Bruce Wilson in a Melbourne house purchased with funds illegally obtained through union fraud. Milne did not check the story with Gillard or her office, and when she protested *The Australian* did apologise and retract the story as well as deleting it from their website. However, the story continued to have an underground half-life, being repeated in various blogs.

In a celebrity-conscious age, where people in the public eye are expected to be engaging, if not actively lovable, Gillard was well aware of her own shortcomings in telling her government's story. Throughout her prime ministership there were constant complaints that she droned on like a lawyer speaking to a brief rather than a prime minister explaining policy to an often sceptical electorate.

She never liked delivering formal speeches, she said – and she pointed out quickly that other Australian prime ministers were not especially good at it either. 'Paul [Keating] was a shocker,' she told me. 'Compared to the sparring Keating having a wonderful go in question time, he was a totally different person. Even in the Redfern speech [made in December 1992 in Sydney's Redfern Park and publicly acknowledging to Aboriginal Australians the disastrous effects European settlement has had on their culture] which is a wonderful speech, half the Indigenous people in the audience didn't know what he was saying until halfway through. He was so unemotional, it wasn't like he grabbed them from the start.

'Howard was the same. I remember right in the middle of 9/11 he gave a press conference and his demeanour was really businesslike. There was nothing emotional in his presentation – rage, tears because so many people had died – and by today's standards people would look at that and say, Talk about cold. If I'd done that press conference, people would have said, God, she's so wooden . . .

'But you see then – with Paul and with John Howard – prime ministers weren't expected to emote. Howard did at various points during his prime ministership, with the gun legislation for instance, and the Bali bombings where he got the father of the nation thing happening, but for most of the time he wasn't expected to perform for the cameras.

'People are much more critical now. I think it's part of the general media backdrop, the politician as celebrity.

'I came to the prime ministership under extraordinary circumstances, but even if I hadn't there was always going to be a fuss about me – first woman PM, what is she going to look like, how do we react about those images. There were sharp judgements made about whether I should be in the job, and about how I presented.

'And I think these judgements about me were

made much faster because of the circumstances, because of my gender and because of the faster media cycle.'

Gillard occasionally allowed people to glimpse her angry and passionate side. The most emotional public speeches she gave – as deputy PM during the Victorian bushfires in February 2009, when attacking Tony Abbott for his sexism and misogyny in October 2012 and speaking to the victims of forced adoption in March 2013 – are galvanising to watch, for they show her speaking from the heart. But the passionate Gillard was not as well known as she should have been, for her preferred forum was Parliament – not usually high on the viewing list of most Australian voters.

Gillard set herself and her government a huge and difficult task: to deliver change. This meant having to explain complex policies and initiatives to a generally resistant voting public, faced by an Opposition leader skilled at crafting memorable and therefore convincing slogans, and in a media landscape not especially skilled at understanding and reporting nuance. (In the case of climate change, for instance, much less attention has been given to evidence that the earth is warming than to arguments about whether this is true or not.) To her prime ministership Gillard brought the skills of a trained lawyer – not a phrasemaker, a rhetorician or an actor. She tried to get voters to understand the issues, what she and her government were trying to do. But slogans and grabs are always quicker and easier – and journalists often go for the easiest stories.

I found her surprisingly sympathetic to journalists in general, with some exceptions. 'Given the media landscape we have, this is not a good time to try and explain complex issues,' she said. 'My view of the media is that journalists are dealing with new technology, job losses in the media industry, and they're trying to accommodate to the pace of change. You see this played out in a lot of tabloid coverage, not only here but right around the world. And the reaction to these changes is more schlock, more drama, more gore, more A versus B, more everything. The news cycle used to be much longer too, but now stories can disappear almost as soon as they're out there.

'I think the public's reaction to this is that there's just too much noise, the volume is increasing, both in bulk and shrillness. There's a superficiality in a lot of media coverage as a result. Readers know it's overblown and become distrustful, and people will start looking for credentialled voices and more quality. People will get their information from a whole variety of different sources, too, because there is just so much. They'll be more selective, but we're not there yet.

'But the fact that there are so many sources of information now, and so many opinions, has problems of its own. Now it's possible to get your information from only, say, climate change sceptics, or other sources that just reinforce one opinion without knowing there is another view. Because there is just so much, people are cutting into it more selectively.

'So the media landscape is bigger and smaller at the same time . . . truly a global village.'[4]

An increasingly important part of the mix is the role of social media. 'I think it's incredibly strong,' she said. 'I don't think we quite understand yet how it's going to change the shape of democracy, not just here but around the world.

'It has the benefit of being able to segment bits of the population. We can target women with kids, have a conversation with young people. Its huge strength is real-time engagement, the sense that you can have the online equivalent of a town meeting anytime, anywhere. I think that's fantastic.

'It's like the community cabinets. I like all of that. I like being able to talk to people unmediated, in direct engagement.

'The cruelty that often goes with anonymity of

course has to be factored into the political conversation, but so much of that is so rabid that sometimes it can be ignored.'

This must have been very difficult for her at times. Julia Gillard undoubtedly attracted more unpleasant, even vitriolic, criticism than any previous Australian prime minister, and much of this has been because of her gender. An enormous amount of attention – approving or hostile – was paid to her appearance: her hairstyle, her voice, her clothes. Germaine Greer's comment on ABC-TV's *Q&A* that Gillard has a 'big arse' made headlines. This kind of scrutiny has been the lot of women in positions of power or traditionally male roles for a long time: Joan of Arc was probably criticised for the cut of her armour. Margaret Thatcher and Hillary Clinton both ignored comments about their appearance, and by and large Julia Gillard has too.

Gillard told commentator Anne Summers that she and Clinton 'shared reflections' about being women in top jobs when they met in Perth late last year. '[Hillary Clinton] said to me that she never really felt the issue about gender when she was a senator. It was when she put herself forward for executive office that she felt it so acutely.' Like Gillard, Clinton had to endure newspaper headlines over a long-resolved matter: in Gillard's case completely spurious rumours about her involvement in union corruption as a result of her liaison with Bruce Wilson; in Clinton's case unfounded suspicions about property dealings and the Whitewater scandal.

Clinton's advice was to try and deal with these matters directly and quickly. 'She said "you don't let it drift, you've got to stand up to it and be clear about it and name it for what it is because the temptation is to say, 'Look, this is so absurd it'll die a death', whereas these things unfortunately don't."' Gillard had already held a press conference at which she spent almost an hour answering every single question thrown at her about the Wilson business. In the end there were no more questions, the conference finished – and several journalists wrote that she still had a case to answer.

Personal attacks were conflated with a lack of respect for the office of prime minister, as if a woman had no right to a man's job. With the government on a sliver-thin majority, conservative opposition turned increasingly disrespectful and even vicious in 2011 and 2012. At an anti-carbon-pricing rally, Tony Abbott appeared in front of posters and placards saying 'ditch the witch' and describing Gillard as 'Bob Brown's bitch', a reference to the Greens' insistence on changes to the carbon pricing policy on which Gillard had compromised in order to retain their support. The Leader of the Opposition also made a point of attacking her sotto voce at the dispatch box. She was regularly addressed as 'Julia' in media interviews, not 'Prime Minister' or 'Ms Gillard'. Shock jock Alan Jones described her as 'Ju-liar'.

The hatred for Julia Gillard occasionally reached a level that now seems almost demented. Retired cartoonist Larry Pickering regularly sent supporters drawings of the prime minister with a strap-on penis or a dominatrix's whip. There were nasty, sexist jokes all over the internet. As Anne Summers observed, Gillard was subjected to a level of sexual harassment that would be illegal in any other workplace.[5]

The message from all this is something many Australians would not wish to admit: that generally lip service is given to the idea of women in power until a woman actually takes power and uses it. Recently a young girl yelled racist abuse at an elite sportsman during a football match and was immediately and widely condemned for it. Middle-aged men repeatedly called the female prime minister vile and sexist names and there was comparatively little media comment.

After enduring almost eighteen months of this, Gillard fought back. On 10 October 2012, the House of Representatives was discussing the issue of former speaker Peter Slipper, then standing aside while the federal court dealt with accusations of sexual harassment brought against him by a former colleague. Tony Abbott had been strong in his condemnation of Slipper – a long-time friend – on the grounds of sexism and misogyny. Given Abbott's continuing behaviour towards her, Julia Gillard decided she had had enough. 'I could not take the hypocrisy of the Leader of the Opposition talking about sexism,' she said. 'I was not going to sit silent.'

Sit silent she did not. For fifteen minutes, beginning with the words: 'I will not be lectured on sexism and misogyny by this man', Julia Gillard gave one of the best parliamentary speeches of her life. Quoting from a dossier of Abbott quotes she found objectionable, she proceeded to take him apart, deliberately and forensically.

'Let's go through the Opposition Leader's repulsive double standards,' she began, icy rage showing in every line of her body. 'He has said, and I quote, in a discussion about women being underrepresented in institutions of power in Australia, "If it's true . . . that men have more power generally speaking than women, is that a bad thing?"

'. . . And then of course it goes on. I was very offended personally when the Leader of the Opposition as minister for health said, and I quote,

"Abortion is the easy way out." You said that in March 2004, I suggest you check the records.

'. . . And now the Leader of the Opposition . . . has decided the speaker is a [sexist and misogynist] because that suits [his] political purpose.

'Doesn't turn a hair about any of his past statements, doesn't walk into this Parliament and apologise to the women of Australia. Doesn't walk into this Parliament and apologise to me for the things that have come out of his mouth. But now seeks to use this as a battering ram against someone else.'

Her gaze drilled into a hunched-down and diminished Tony Abbott. Recalling the words of Alan Jones that her recently deceased and much-loved father had died of shame at having such a daughter, a comment recalled by Abbott himself in his preceding speech, she added: 'The government is not dying of shame, *my father did not die of shame*, what the Opposition Leader should be ashamed of is his performance in this parliament and the sexism he brings with it.' She ended with: 'The Leader of the Opposition should think seriously about the role of women in public life and in Australian society, because we are entitled to a better standard than this.'

Gillard thought this was just another fiery speech in Parliament. She told me, 'I wasn't expecting to give a speech, but I was ready to have a red-hot go at the Leader of the Opposition. I thought I had given a hard-hitting speech but I didn't have any inkling of the effect of it.'

So unaware was she of what she had done that when she swung her chair around to Wayne Swan, she told him: 'Oh, we're going to have to sit here now and listen to all these bloody speeches in reply. I should get my chief of staff to bring some correspondence so at least I can be getting on with something.

'And Wayne, with a slightly odd look on his face, and he is not someone known for the most demonstrative facial expressions, said, "Yeah, you can't really give the 'I accuse' speech and settle back and do your correspondence."'

Swan was right. Very quickly the speech went viral on social media, and not just in Australia. Many women of all ages felt that Julia Gillard was speaking for them. The *New Yorker* praised Gillard's speech in a blog post, favourably comparing Gillard's passion with President Obama's perceived lack of it. Gillard's speech was the subject of a question on BBC Radio 4's *News Quiz* program. It was mentioned in the *New York Times*, in *The Guardian* and elsewhere, and always favourably.

Except in Canberra. Australian media commentators lined up to condemn Gillard's speech as shrill, over the top, flawed and desperate. They also said her attack on Tony Abbott was a defence of Peter Slipper, a failure to attack him, and a cynical ploy to divert attention from the problems of the former speaker. (In her speech Gillard said, 'I am offended . . . but I also believe . . . that this Parliament should recognise that there is a court case in progress. That the judge has reserved his decision, that having waited for a number of months for the legal matters surrounding Mr Slipper to come to a conclusion, that the Parliament should see that conclusion.')

In a later interview she took strong exception to the suggestion that she had in effect been whingeing. 'How do you get yourself there?' she asked. 'Does that mean that people shouldn't stand up for their rights and [instead] just . . . be there silent?'[6] This is true, of course. It would have been good, however, if more of her colleagues had stuck up for her, supported her position.

Gillard's attack on Tony Abbott and misogyny, with its final passionate 'we are entitled to a better standard than this', may yet become a haiku for Gillard's prime ministership, an encapsulation of what she stood for, or perhaps simply the verbal marker of a significant moment in Australia's national consciousness, like John Howard's 'we will choose who comes to this country and the circumstances under which they come' or Paul Keating's 'this is the recession we had to have'. Gillard herself seemed surprised, though no doubt also grimly pleased, that what she said resonated so strongly for so many people, and not only women.

As Paul Keating once observed, the way of the reformer is difficult in Australia. Governments who try to do big things are usually hammered at the ballot box, though history generally sheds a kinder light on them. That is undoubtedly because historians' evaluations do not depend on a government's success in manipulating the daily news cycle in getting their message out to the electorate.

Gillard's government had many good news stories, but Labor supporters were often frustrated by their presentation to the public. One supporter I know put it this way: 'Their motto should be, "We've done some good things, we're just not very good at telling you about them".'

Both in Opposition and in government, Julia Gillard spent hours of her political life doing deals, talking to various stakeholders in small rooms, understanding different and often opposing points of view, arguing, working out compromises. She was good at crafting policies acceptable to a range of stakeholders. But she was much less adept at seeing how such decisions would play out in the perception of the voters. There is a case for describing the Gillard government as a competent administration led by a less-than-great salesman versus a pretty ordinary Opposition led by an excellent one.

More than once Gillard's government picked fights with powerful vested interests, antagonising them and muddying public perception of what the government was trying to achieve. Two examples of many were the botched mining tax and the government's attempts to introduce stronger media regulation and squibbing the result, thereby irritating both powerful media interests and members of the public who approved of the proposed changes in the first place.

Some journalists asked, What happened to the consensus model that the Hawke government followed with so much success during the 1980s? The ability to get big reforms through with a minimum of conflict? Gillard would have none of that. 'I think there's been a lot of reinterpreting of history,' she said. 'I don't recall Paul Keating in the 1993 election campaign, in the fight of his life against the GST, looking for the consensus moment.' (She was being a little disingenuous: Keating realised that he could make political capital and possibly win an election by opposing the GST, which he privately supported. There are better examples: Hawke and the 1989 pilots' strike is one.) 'Government in my view isn't about looking at the powerful stakeholders and saying, "How many can I get in my corner?" Government is about serving the national interest and doing what the nation requires.'[7]

For three years Gillard worked with a lot of lead in her saddlebags. But she placed some of that lead there herself, through misguided communication, less than adroit political timing and some decisions that needlessly antagonised sections of the electorate.

The message itself was not always well chosen, either. Under the Rudd and Gillard governments Australia successfully dodged the bullet of the global financial crisis; inflation is currently low, employment high. According to one measure, since 2007 Labor created more than 960000 jobs. Australia's economic prosperity is envied by many other countries: we have not had a recession for twenty years. These things did not happen by accident, but as the result of good economic decisions and prudent financial management carried out by both conservative and Labor governments over the past forty years, and built on by the Rudd and Gillard governments.

Clouds are gathering, certainly, but Australia is still in a better economic position than almost any other Western country.

Gillard and treasurer Wayne Swan, however, did not point this out very strongly, choosing instead to insist that Australians are doing it tough. By taking this approach they implicitly acknowledged that Australians like to believe that they are taxed too heavily and to grumble about the government. The country's success in dodging three previous recessions has made some feel that they cannot have been so bad, overseas experiences to the contrary. Not dealing effectively with this perception has meant almost nullifying some of Labor and Gillard's most significant achievements.

Gillard did a great deal for financially disadvantaged Australians: the National Disability Insurance Scheme; increases in the tax-free threshold, pensions and superannuation; child care rebates; measures to make aged care easier and more affordable. However, she has also ruled that single parents would not continue to receive the relatively generous supporting parents' benefit as soon as their child turned eight: if they did not find a job they would receive the much smaller Newstart allowance (i.e. the dole).

This was a modest correction to the Howard government policy that only parents applying for the benefit were affected by this rule: those already receiving it could keep it for another eight years. Gillard's policy put all supporting single parents in the same boat. Intended to save money and move people into the workforce, this measure made many believe that a cruel government was penalising single parents, mostly women. The announcement of this policy at roughly the same time as Gillard made her widely approved misogyny speech did not help: Gillard had to wear the accusations that she, Australia's first woman prime minister, had betrayed disadvantaged women.

Gillard's social conservatism was sometimes at odds with apparent political sense. In the face of several governments around the world changing the law to accept gay marriage, she consistently refused to do so, citing the provisions of the Marriage Act in true lawyerly fashion. Eventually the level of protest within the ALP grew to the point where gay marriage was voted as party policy, and Gillard allowed a conscience vote on the subject – though, given the Opposition's view, an amendment to the act would be unlikely to go through. Gay marriage is the kind of issue that, while it directly affects a relatively small area of the population, has much greater resonance in terms of perceived discrimination against a minority. For a Labor prime minister to support it would have been a good move, attracting wide approval at no political cost. But Gillard did not see this.

Another perceived error was Gillard's 'captain's pick' of former Olympian Nova Peris as the Northern Territory's top-of-the-ticket Senate candidate for the 2013 election. Its aim might have been laudable – to have a high-profile Aboriginal woman in the Senate for the first time – but ALP members and stakeholders in the Northern Territory, including the long-serving senator whom Peris would replace, protested that the decision had been hastily made without consultation, and was yet another example of Canberra arrogance.

Another unforced error was Gillard's endorsement of Victorian powerbroker David Feeney as preferred candidate for Gellibrand, the very safe Labor seat vacated by former attorney-general Nicola Roxon, instead of a woman. This was harmful in two ways: it led to questioning of Gillard's feminist credentials, especially as the woman candidate had been chosen by Emily's List, of which Gillard is a member. And secondly, David Feeney was one of the ALP powerbrokers who had come to Gillard in June 2010 to ask her to stand against Kevin Rudd. Choosing him looked like payback for services rendered.

There were times when Gillard's choice of words was unfortunate. She commented that 457 temporary visas for skilled workers were being abused to put 'foreign workers' at the head of the queue. Gillard defended her words, going for the substance rather than the perceived xenophobic message of what she had said: 'I'm a Labor prime minister talking about jobs . . . The 457 visa system is a short-term temporary visa for skills shortages. If it's being used for any other purpose by anyone, then it's being used wrongly and we should stamp it out.' Her implied criticism of 'foreigners' attracted an approving comment from Pauline Hanson, surely not something Gillard thought she had invited or would have welcomed.

Gillard argued that these and other political mistakes are matters of perception, questions of spin or what she calls 'over-interpretation'. But the fact that she made them at all indicated a certain lack of engagement with the electorate. This came about for several reasons: sometimes-hostile media spin, her own occasional impulsiveness and impatience to get things done, her focus on results, her own life experience as a single woman who has spent her working life in the law and in politics. However, while claiming kinship with working-class Australians in the suburbs – the so-called Howard's battlers who lost their jobs and deserted the ALP in droves during the 1991 recession and whom the ALP must win back in order to retain government – Gillard was not good at couching her government's policies in terms that would appeal to them, despite the reformist nature of many things she did and her emphasis on the twin themes of opportunity and access. She also missed many opportunities for showing leadership. In discussing the National Disability Insurance Scheme, she emphasised its practical results, the this-could-happen-to-any-of-us side of this landmark policy. More effectively, she could have said that the NDIS was necessary because we are a society that looks after our less fortunate: this is what Australians do.

Perception depends much more heavily on emotion than on fact, and part of a prime minister's job is to reflect back the hopes and aspirations of the people. Politics can be seen as a form of national storytelling, and Gillard was not a natural storyteller. She was a solver of problems, an answerer of questions. Her government tended to make large announcements without necessarily preparing the electorate to hear them, to initiate change without much warning at a time when many people were facing uncertainty, coming to terms with new employment rules and practices, as well as global warming and changes brought about by technology. All these things fed into the perception of many voters that Gillard and her government could not be trusted.

Julia Gillard came to office at a time when, despite an electorate that enjoys the highest levels of education in Australian history, there was a growing aversion to complexity, a lack of willingness to listen to nuanced arguments. Simplicity is easier to understand and to accept, for – as Tony Abbott exploited with great success – it is easier to say 'no' than to think about issues. Gillard said, 'He knows how to frame a campaign around complaint. What he's got no vision for, and no self-belief in, is a campaign around what you can construct – and I don't think a campaign around complaint gets you there.'[8]

She agreed with former British PM Tony Blair that politics all across the Western world is a much more brutal business now than in the past. Perception lives and dies by opinion polls, and almost from the time it came into office the Gillard government was in the doldrums.

'I get it [with polls] and why they eat so much media attention,' she told me. 'But the choice at the end of the day isn't what you tell the nice person from Nielsen when they ring you up. It's what you do when you mark that ballot paper, when all the noise has died down and there is effectively a binary choice for who leads the nation, and you ask yourself who has got the personal capabilities to do it.

'When the history of the time is written, it's only

the political aficionados who remember what the opinion polls were doing at the time. People don't write the story of Hawke opening up the modern economy against the backdrop of opinion polls. They write about policy measures.

'Societies are shaped not by what is happening on the surface, but by the great tidal movements underneath.'

Ruddmanship

In terms of speed and efficiency, the removal of Kevin Rudd as prime minister in 2010 was highly successful, like the invasion of Iraq. However, like the invasion of Iraq, the consequences were unpredictable, and did not include greater stability.

The first was immediate: an inexorable stream of newspaper and TV stories about Rudd's possible return to the top job, with opinion polls indicating he was much more popular with the public than the woman who had toppled him. None of this seemed to bother Julia Gillard greatly, for she drew strength and authority from a fact that many of her critics either did not know or ignored: the prime minister is the leader of the party that has won office, and he or she is chosen by colleagues, not by the voters. Gillard knew she had the support of her colleagues.

It apparently made little difference to the commentariat that the Labor Caucus had indicated their lack of enthusiasm for Kevin Rudd.

However, the will-Rudd-come-back speculation refused to go away – not least because for many journalists leadership stories inject some much-needed drama into the daily grind of reporting from Canberra. These stories have been a major source of media movement and colour for years: Hawke v Hayden (1982), Hawke v Keating (1991), Beazley v Crean (2001 and 2003), Latham v Beazley (2003), Beazley v Rudd (2006). The Gillard–Rudd conflict, however, was like the constant speculation about Keating taking over from Hawke in the late 1980s, the Howard–Peacock conflicts of the 1990s, and the interminable saga of John Howard and Peter Costello that continued throughout Howard's prime ministership. These were low-level stories that, like Gillard v Rudd, were the journalistic gifts that kept on giving.

During the 2010 election campaign, various journalists – notably Laurie Oakes – reported damaging details about what happened on the night that Gillard challenged Rudd for the leadership, information designed to give the impression that she had made a ruthless grab for power at the behest of a few powerbrokers. It is now presumed, with reason, that these leaks came from Rudd himself, or at least that he encouraged them. As time passed, Rudd adopted another equally deliberate strategy. Whenever the polls indicated that Julia Gillard's popularity levels were rising slightly, whether because of a policy initiative or some other factor, Rudd would allow himself to be interviewed, usually with some mildly expressed and self-deprecating criticism of the government. When she made a mistake there he was again, more in sorrow than in anger. *Sydney Morning Herald* cartoonist Alan Moir once drew Gillard making a speech with dozens of beaming little Kevin Rudds popping up all round her.

In public Rudd, who had asked for and been given the job of minister for foreign affairs after June 2010, played the role of a good sport, insisting that his main focus was his new job, and that he would concentrate on that while doing his best to ensure the defeat of Tony Abbott. This could have been interpreted as support for Gillard and her team, but at no point did he say that he had given up on the possibility of being prime minister again, and he never discouraged journalists from asking about that either.

Nobody thought to ask how the prime ministership of a resurgent Rudd would differ from the approaches Gillard had been taking, especially as she was carrying out many of the policy initiatives that had been crafted under his leadership. But Rudd did not appear to be considering any new agendas.

Not long after Rudd was deposed, stories began to circulate in the press and elsewhere about his leadership: stories that had long been known in Canberra, but details of which were being made public for the first time. Gillard confirmed what she had hinted when she took over the prime ministership: that under Rudd the Cabinet's decision-making process had stalled. Massive issues had needed resolving: how to handle the emissions trading scheme after its parliamentary defeat; a response to the Henry taxation review; hospital reform; the mining tax. Rudd and his inner circle, which did not always include his close Cabinet colleagues Wayne Swan and Julia Gillard, had travelled around the country, holding meetings and speaking to people without translating all that into effective and workable policy initiatives.

This indecisive way of working had been evident from the early days of Rudd's prime ministership. It was one reason why, when he was overseas, long queues formed outside Julia Gillard's office door: people knew she was a lot more efficient and able to make decisions.

Gillard and her Cabinet colleagues had also been concerned about, and often exasperated by, Rudd's centralised way of working. He turned more and more to his personal office, sometimes giving his bright young staff responsibilities they were not qualified or sufficiently experienced to handle. In status-conscious Canberra, this was a further cause of resentment, as well as leading to concerns about the practice of good governance.

Many observers still cannot understand why Kevin Rudd's colleagues had been unable to rein him in, why it took them so long to do something about him. Perhaps nobody wanted to rock the boat, especially as the voters apparently liked him so much: his poll ratings were consistently high for a long time. Whatever the reasons, Julia Gillard and her colleagues were managing, though through gritted teeth, to get their jobs done, to manoeuvre around the Rudd roadblock.

For a busy government with a huge and challenging agenda – for a deputy who knew how to run her office and who did so quietly and competently – Rudd's approach must have been difficult to handle. But the government's front bench and Rudd's other colleagues did such a good job of hiding this, and for so long, that when things came to a head in June 2010, hardly anyone outside Parliament knew about it.

It is interesting to compare the Rudd way of dealing

with his deposition with that adopted by John Howard in 1989, when he lost the Liberal Party leadership to Andrew Peacock. This was when Howard made his famous comment that for him to stage a comeback would be like 'Lazarus with a triple bypass'. He kept resolutely quiet for five and a half years, confident that the times would suit him eventually, and he came back to the party leadership, winning the 1996 election against Paul Keating. Howard knew how to wait, to bide his time: Rudd, enjoying the publicity and the media hype, reminded everybody that he was there at every possible opportunity.

After the events of June 2010, Gillard and Rudd were punctiliously polite to each other in their public and professional dealings. But Gillard could hardly have been unaware of what was happening behind her back. She had always known that some members of her government were less than wholehearted supporters of hers, and Rudd was cultivating these MPs, who helped his cause along by criticising some of her decisions. Regular newspaper readers and followers of parliamentary politics soon learned to read between the lines, and so to discover who some of these disaffected MPs were.

Matters came to a head in February 2012. On the 21st, Rudd, who was in Washington, DC, very publicly resigned as foreign minister, stating that he could no longer continue without Gillard's support. He said he had been forced to step down because he had been attacked by 'Labor faceless men'. Gillard, he said, had chosen not to discipline her colleagues for their attacks, and therefore he believed that she shared their views. He did not say whether he intended to challenge for the leadership or to resign from parliament – the latter a course of action that would have given the Gillard government a by-election, which was the last thing they wanted.

He did not tell Gillard of his intention to resign before he made his decision, and she expressed formal regret and disappointment without going into more in public than that. (She has resolutely refused to comment on 'the conduct of any individuals'[1].)

The situation was too much for her supporters, especially deputy prime minister and treasurer Wayne Swan. Just before Rudd returned to Australia Swan released a statement to the media: 'Prime Minister Gillard and I and the overwhelming majority of our colleagues have been applying our Labor values to the policy challenges in front of us, and we're succeeding despite tremendous political obstacles. For the sake of the labour movement, the government and the Australians which it represents, we have refrained from criticism to date.

'However, for too long Kevin Rudd has been putting his own self-interest ahead of the interests of the broader labour movement and the country as a whole, and that needs to stop. The Party has given Kevin Rudd all the opportunities in the world, and he wasted them with his dysfunctional decision-making and his deeply demeaning attitude towards other people, including our Caucus colleagues . . .

'Julia . . . is delivering major reforms and getting things done that her predecessor could not. Colleagues are sick of Kevin Rudd driving the vote down by sabotaging policy announcements and undermining our substantial economic successes. The Labor Party is not about a person. It's about a purpose. That's something Prime Minister Gillard has always known in her heart but something Kevin Rudd has never understood.'[2]

It was an unforgiving assessment by a man who had known Rudd for more than thirty years, ever since they were at Nambour State High School together. Swan, normally the most mild-mannered of men, at least in public, was widely criticised for what he wrote, but it is reasonable to assume that he echoed the sentiments of many of his colleagues, possibly also including Gillard, though she would not have chosen to go public as he had done. Of course, this did not increase stability.

Rudd now challenged Gillard for the leadership,

and she accepted. Anthony Albanese, the leader of the government in the House of Representatives, gave an emotional press conference in which he declared his support for Rudd. He said he had offered Gillard his resignation as manager of government business, which she had refused to accept – a signal that she did not want to contribute to the bloodletting any more than she had to. It meant that Albanese was still able to work on Rudd's behalf.

On the morning of 27 February 2012, grim-faced members of the ALP parliamentary party filed into the Caucus room for the ballot, while journalists waited breathlessly down the corridor. It did not take long: Gillard won by 71 votes to 31. Not long afterwards, Rudd faced the press, reiterating his intention to work tirelessly from the backbench for the government's victory over Tony Abbott at the next election. He took no questions and retired to the backbench.

A few days later on 2 March, Gillard announced that Rudd had been replaced as foreign minister, and by another Labor star, former NSW premier Bob Carr. Gillard had long maintained friendly connections with the Carr circle – her chief of staff, Amanda Lampe, had been one of Carr's press secretaries – and by all accounts Bob Carr was her personal choice for the job, despite his lack of foreign policy experience.

Carr's appointment was hailed as a good idea by most of the media, even a masterstroke. It certainly gave the third most senior position in Cabinet to a new face, to an experienced Labor man who was not obviously aligned to either Gillard or Rudd. It was widely regarded as a signal of Gillard's desire to make a fresh start, though at the same time it put a few more experienced noses out of joint.

Three months earlier in December 2011 Gillard had expanded the number of Cabinet ministers by two to twenty-two, promoting Tanya Plibersek, Mark Butler and Bill Shorten. That reshuffle gained quite a lot of media attention. Reshuffles usually attract some comment, usually about the competence and possible performance of the newly promoted. But this time speculation was couched in terms of punishment and reward for the roles of various ministers in the toppling of Kevin Rudd eighteen months before. Journalists pointed out that Bill Shorten, the new workplace relations and employment minister, and Mark Arbib, newly promoted to assistant treasurer, had been prominent backers of Gillard against Rudd. In the same reshuffle, industry minister Kim Carr was demoted from Cabinet, becoming minister in charge of manufacturing and defence materiel, and he made clear that the change of portfolio had not been of his choosing.

Kim Carr's relationship with Gillard had always been a wary one. A powerbroker of the Victorian Left, he had actively moved against her early attempts to gain preselection. Later, when he and Gillard were both in Parliament, they had established a workable professional connection, and in 2006 he had brokered the deal that enabled Rudd and Gillard to combine forces against Kim Beazley and his deputy Jenny Macklin and to take over the leadership of the parliamentary ALP, then in Opposition.

Gillard had always been aware that Carr was not a wholehearted supporter of hers, and indeed when he had to choose between Gillard and Rudd in June 2010, he had gone with Rudd. His demotion from her inner circle – he retained the manufacturing portfolio but was to work under climate change and industry minister Greg Combet – was a tough, pragmatic decision on Gillard's part, and one that had consequences. It attracted some criticism, with union and industry sources declaring that by demoting Carr Gillard had downgraded the importance of the manufacturing industry, a claim Gillard denied. Carr himself said the reshuffle did not reflect 'our efforts and achievements', but added, in reference to his new role, but possibly not referring to that alone, 'We have unfinished business.'[3] Robert McClelland, a Rudd supporter demoted in the same reshuffle, moving from attorney-general to emergency services and housing, also stated that he would have preferred to stay in his former job.

On 5 March 2012, after defeating Rudd and only three months after the previous reshuffle, Gillard made further changes. Gillard supporter Brendan O'Connor became minister for small business, and – in a more surprising development – David Bradbury replaced Mark Arbib as assistant treasurer, for Arbib announced that he had decided to resign as a senator and minister. One of the Labor powerbrokers derided by Rudd as 'faceless men' in June 2010, he gave the usual reasons for his resignation: to spend time with his family and to help the party heal. It was never clear whether Gillard asked for his resignation, but his departure at least stopped speculation about whether he had been rewarded or not.

Robert McClelland relinquished his emergency services portfolio and his Cabinet spot and went to the backbench. It is fair to assume that he did so with about as much enthusiasm as when he had left his position as attorney-general. McClelland came from an old Labor family: his father had been Senator Doug McClelland, manager of government business in the Senate and minister for media under Gough Whitlam, and president of the senate under Bob

Hawke. Robert McClelland later announced that he would not stand for re-election in 2013.

Gillard's reshuffle decisions were hailed by some as prudent and sensible and proof that she had faced down her pro-Rudd enemies within the party, and by others as further evidence that the federal parliamentary party was in a state of crisis and disarray. But Gillard must have known that the problem of Kevin Rudd was not about to go away. He and his supporters might have lost power but they were still there, on the backbench. It is worth noting that none of them resigned their seats: presumably nobody wanted to be held responsible for the downfall of a Labor government by causing a difficult by-election. They just stayed on the backbench and waited.

For the rest of that year there were various 'damaging leaks' from 'Labor insiders' about instability in the government and discontent in the ranks of the parliamentary ALP. Rudd continued his tactic of bobbing up to comment on something Gillard had done or failed to do. And this is more or less how things stood until the third week of March 2013.

At various stages of consideration before Parliament that month was a huge range of legislation. It included the National Disability Insurance Scheme, pensions and welfare benefits, the position of Hazara refugees in Australia, eradicating asbestos from old buildings, extensions of the Sex Discrimination Act, the ability of Australian workers to negotiate more flexible working arrangements, the compulsory licensing of financial advisers, the use of Tax Office records to update electoral rolls, and environmental strictures on coal seam gas operators. It may be that in that week the Gillard government set a new record for the number of things accomplished.

The week probably also set a record for the number of national issues almost totally ignored by the mainstream media. For this was the week of another Rudd leadership challenge.

For some days there had been rumblings that Kevin Rudd might move against Gillard again: Gillard and Rudd neither confirmed nor denied them, with Gillard calmly concentrating on getting her legislation through. Late on the morning of 21 March, she led a bipartisan apology to mothers and children separated by forced adoption, her words both moving and heartfelt. It was one of her best speeches.

But except for those directly concerned, this event had little immediate public resonance. Shortly after 1 p.m. a solemn Simon Crean, minister for the arts and regional development, a member of Cabinet and one of Gillard's longtime supporters, called a press conference. He spoke slowly, choosing his words carefully. 'It seems to me that the party through the government is in a stalemate position,' he said. 'Something needs to be done to break the deadlock, to resolve the issue once and for all, and to enable us to get on with the job we were actually elected to do, that is to campaign on behalf of the Australian people for Labor values.' Voters could be pardoned for feeling faintly bewildered by this: why was Crean suddenly talking about 'deadlock'?

Crean continued, 'I am asking [the PM] to call a spill of all leadership positions in the party. I will not be standing for the leader, I will be putting myself forward in the leadership team for the deputy leader . . . This is an issue that has to be resolved, there is too much at stake . . . this is not personal.

'Kevin Rudd in my view has no alternative but to stand for the leadership.' Crean ended by saying that people didn't want Tony Abbott as prime minister, but they were fed up with 'us' at the moment. He hoped that what he said would be a circuit-breaker and give the party some 'clear air'.

In an interview Crean later gave journalist Kate Legge[4], he outlined some of the things that had disturbed him about Gillard's leadership: Gillard's choice of Nova Peris for a Northern Territory Senate spot without proper party consultation, the reshuffle after the resignations of attorney-general Nicola Roxon and Senate leader Chris Evans in February 2013, Gillard's handling of the 457 visa issue, her determination to put 'Australians ahead of foreigners'.

But clearly the overall public perception of Gillard's government was what most worried Crean. As he told Legge, 'When people come to you scratching their heads and we keep going down in the polls because we've made bad decisions and we're not getting our message out, you come to the conclusion that you need the circuit-breaker because you've got to stop the destabilisation and start giving people the case for wanting to vote Labor again.'

Gillard and Crean had been friends for fifteen years, ever since Gillard entered parliament in 1998. She had gone on holiday with him and his family; she had publicly defended him when he was the embattled leader of the Opposition in 2002; he had given Gillard her first opportunities to prove herself as a politician.

Gillard was predictably guarded in her comments about Crean.[5] She said, 'I was very upset that he had made that decision, and what it would mean for our friendship. Simon and I had this sense of bonding, we believe in the same things, we've had a good relationship over time. But this tremendously difficult thing happened . . . I don't know why he did what he did. But as well as being upset I felt a real sense of frustration and sadness for Simon, because I knew it was going to end badly for him.' Her anger and frustration were no doubt assuaged by the knowledge that she continued to be supported by the greater part of Caucus.

When Gillard was faced with unpleasant and difficult decisions, she didn't usually shirk them, and she did not now. Almost immediately she asked for Simon Crean's resignation. He told Kate Legge, 'I said, "This outcome has not been determined . . . If it goes the other way then you can have my resignation." That's when she said, "I'm terminating it now."' And so, to the shock of his friend Martin Ferguson and other colleagues, Crean went straight to the backbench at the start of the next question time. Ferguson wondered, 'How could she do that, after all you've done for her?' obviously not taking into account what Crean had done for Gillard that day.

During Crean's press conference, he said he doubted Gillard would agree to call a spill. He was wrong. At the beginning of question time, an icily defiant prime minister announced that there would be a leadership spill at 4.30 that afternoon. 'In the meantime,' she added, 'take your best shot,' and sat down amid an outbreak of surprised laughter. An

Opposition attempt to move a motion of no confidence in the government was defeated.

On a normal Thursday afternoon at the end of a parliamentary sitting week, Canberra airport is a sea of corporate clothing as MPs prepare to leave the national capital for their electorates. Not that week: Labor MPs and their staff hit the phones. Twitter went mad, with journalists speculating on Rudd's numbers and Labor MPs declaring their allegiance one way or the other. Commentators, including former ALP senator Graham Richardson, lost little time in declaring that Rudd would win in a canter, an opinion backed up by the betting agency Sportsbet.

But the big question was whether Rudd would stand against Gillard. Less than an hour before the vote, reports were that he was still undecided, with speculation that he simply did not have the numbers. And then, about ten minutes before Caucus met, Rudd fronted the press. Looking solemn and studious, he said he would not stand for the leadership. 'I believe in honouring my word . . . the only circumstances under which I would consider a return to leadership is if the overwhelming majority of the party requested my return and the position was vacant. Those circumstances do not exist. I will be adhering to the commitment I gave to the Australian people and to my colleagues . . . I take my word seriously.'

Half an hour later, Gillard and Wayne Swan were elected unopposed and unanimously by the Caucus as prime minister and deputy. The whole challenge had been a fizzer. Crean could be pardoned for feeling bitter that Rudd had hung him out to dry: common sense suggests that he would not have declared himself so firmly had he not felt that Rudd was up for the challenge. He later described Rudd as 'spineless'. But Crean's actions were confused at best – it was difficult to see how he could have portrayed himself as the party's circuit-breaker when he was inviting the destabilisation of a leadership vote. However, he had told friends he believed that, as deputy, he could have controlled Rudd and perhaps made him change his style.

It had been an expensive delusion. Gillard says, 'The whole thing ended far worse for Simon than I could ever have guessed, because it never got to the starter's gate. And Simon has had such a long and meritorious political career, and I knew this episode would always influence how that career was remembered.'

A small, grim procession of pro-Rudd MPs went to the prime minister's office to tender their resignations as ministers. They included Chris Bowen, Martin Ferguson, Joel Fitzgibbon and Ed Husic, two senior ministers and two government whips, as well as Parliamentary secretary Richard Marles. Also gone from the frontbench was Kim Carr: seeing him go was probably not a profound cause for regret on Gillard's part.

Gillard replaced her former ministers, bringing Gary Gray and Jason Clare into the Cabinet and combining several portfolios and departments. In terms of policy, perhaps the most significant change was combining the departments of climate change and industry.

The whole leadership episode was, predictably, described as a debacle by most of the media commentators – a further example of Gillard's incompetence and the shambolic nature of the ALP government. After all, as many pointed out, this had been the third ministerial reshuffle in less than a year, complete with amalgamation of various departments and changes of portfolio.

However, an alternative view – and one expressed by several, including former Labor leader Mark Latham – was that Gillard had now successfully seen off most of the frontbench dead wood, and neutralised her enemies. About the only unanimously positive comment Gillard drew was praise for her toughness and refusal to buckle, qualities that, for a woman, and especially one with power, are generally ambiguous at best.

Friendships, alliances and enmities obviously have particular resonance in the hermetic and pressured atmosphere of Parliament. Gillard says that the precise dynamics are difficult to explain, but she describes a party in power as being 'a bit like a family'[6]. It is an unexpectedly cosy comparison until you remember what a family actually is: a group of often widely divergent people brought together by circumstance, some of whom are loving or friendly or pleasant, others unsympathetic, stupid or devious, still others who are unbearable.

There are long and sometimes complex back stories in most of Gillard's decisions about her ministers. However, Mark Latham wrote that her last reshuffle was based on sound principles, pointing out that in the case of other leaders facing a more sympathetic media, her demotion of those who sought to undermine her leadership would have been considered a famous victory. He said Gillard was divesting the party of Labor's 'internal ruling class' – Crean, Ferguson, Joel Fitzgibbon and Robert McClelland are all sons of MPs and ministers from former Labor governments – and promoting new talent in its place. He pointed out that for the first time since 1983 the ALP frontbench was free of second-generation MPs. Gillard, he said was not bound by outmoded ALP tradition. 'Contrary to the right-wing media stereotype, Gillard is her own person.'[7]

In the minds of some of Rudd's erstwhile Caucus colleagues, in the mind of Gillard herself, the events of 21 March served only to confirm what they had already learned about Kevin Rudd: that for the sake of his own ambition, for the sake of his own media profile, he would allow, even encourage, chaos and instability while at the same time clambering onto the moral high ground and thus keeping himself above the fray. For other Caucus members who were being told in poll after poll that they and the government were doomed unless they switched leaders, memories of Rudd's tactics and general unpleasantness began to recede in the face of the necessity for self-preservation. More and more, Julia Gillard found herself battling two opposition parties: one on the other side of the parliamentary chamber, the other behind her.

In the ensuing three months the chatter about forthcoming Rudd challenges did not go away. Labor sank further in the polls, with some showing that the forthcoming election, to be held on 14 September, would not simply be a defeat for the Gillard Labor government: it would be a wipeout of historic proportions.

Media calls for Gillard to step down became more

frequent, even strident, with even *The Age* editorialising on 22 June that Gillard needed to go.[8] In a video interview *Age* editor-in-chief Andrew Holden explained this extraordinary step on the grounds that the newspaper's polls and other sources had confirmed the view that, while voters supported many ALP policies, they had stopped listening to Gillard herself. Voters despaired of the uncertainty and the backbiting within the government, though *The Age* said the paper was more worried about the vacuum in policy debate.

Though *The Age* said they were not entirely convinced that Kevin Rudd had learned his lesson, they said they could not ignore the clear and consistent evidence of the opinion polls that his return to the leadership would enhance Labor's electoral prospects. Labor needed to find the will to make change, to minimise the apparently inevitable damage in September.

Whether or not this particular article was the last straw, four days later, on 26 June, Gillard announced that a leadership ballot for the Party would be held at 7 p.m. that evening. In an interview with Sky News, she added that if she lost the ballot, she would leave parliament and politics, resigning at the next election. She added that she would expect Kevin Rudd to do the same thing, and he had agreed.

The feverish lobbying, the headcounting, the telephoning, began again: this was the fourth time in three years. And as before the big question was whether Kevin Rudd would challenge. And what of the others' allegiances: would Gillard's loyal supporter Bill Shorten stay with her, or would he move to Rudd? What about the women ministers? Rumours flew.

Then Rudd declared he would stand, and Shorten publicly declared for him.

At about 7.35 p.m. it was all over. By a twelve vote margin – 57 to 45 – Julia Gillard was defeated by Kevin Rudd, and her term as prime minister came to an end. This happened on the same day that her Gonski school funding reforms were passed by the Senate.

‘Chasing popularity is the death of purpose’

Among the more dismal results of parliamentary leadership challenges is the departure of other players in the central drama, with measurable collateral damage to the party. Kevin Rudd’s successful challenge to Julia Gillard heralded a parade of departing MPs, who took with them a great deal of expertise and experience. This time, though, it was Gillard’s prominent supporters who left – several of whom had, as members of the front bench, driven some significant and much-needed reforms.

Wayne Swan, treasurer since 2007, Gillard’s deputy during her prime ministership and a consistent and vocal critic of Kevin Rudd, went to the backbench. Stephen Smith, the WA minister for defence who had been foreign minister under Kevin Rudd and who had vacated that portfolio in Rudd’s favour in 2010, announced that he would not stand for re-election, as did Craig Emerson, who resigned as trade minister. Stephen Conroy quit Cabinet and his portfolio as minister for communications, retiring to the backbench. Also refusing to work with Kevin Rudd were minister for agriculture Joe Ludwig and education minister Peter Garrett. A particularly dispiriting departure from federal politics was that of Greg Combet, the former ACTU secretary who, as minister for climate change, had played a key role in one of the Gillard government's most contentious areas.

Those who expected Simon Crean to be returned to Cabinet because he had supported Kevin Rudd were surprised when he too announced that – after more than twenty years as a frontbencher in Opposition and in government – he was retiring at the forthcoming election.

In terms of political theatre, two of the great moments that often define leaders are the way they take power and how they relinquish it when defeated. In the last forty years, television has given Australians ample opportunity to observe this. Gough Whitlam and Bob Hawke came to office triumphant and left it sombre: Malcolm Fraser, who had seemed stony and remote as leader, lost his composure in tears when he conceded defeat. Keating was low key, almost shy, when he became prime minister and, whatever his private feelings, his farewell speech was brief and matter-of-fact. Kevin Rudd, whose image included being the bright kid who was there to help, looked utterly devastated when his party rejected him in 2010.

Julia Gillard's farewell speech, delivered late in the evening of 26 June, was similarly memorable. She was composed and dry-eyed, though her eyes were puffy and a little strained. Perhaps she spoke more quickly than usual, though she never gave the impression that she wanted to get the speech over with. Her words were matter of fact, practical and even gracious: as usual free of soaring rhetoric. She didn't need that. And, as perhaps she had not done often enough during her three years and three days as prime minister, she spoke from the heart.

'In the years in which I've served as prime minister, predominantly, I have faced a minority Parliament and faced internal division within my political party,' she said. 'It has not been an easy environment to work in. But I am pleased that in this environment, which wasn't easy, I have prevailed to ensure that this country is made stronger and smarter and fairer for the future.

'I am very proud of what this government has achieved, which will endure for the long term. Very proud of the way in which we achieved health reform, against the odds, with newly elected conservative leaders. Very pleased that we pushed through and put a price on carbon . . . [which] required us to have the guts and tenacity to stare down one of the most reckless fear campaigns in this nation's history.

'What we have achieved through Disability Care to launch on 1 July this year – apparently an obvious reform to everyone now but something that it took this Labor government to get done, and I am very proud of it.

'I am very proud too of the work we have done in Australian schools . . . It has been the defining passion of my life that every Australian child gets a great opportunity at a life of work and the dignity that comes with work. . .'

Gillard also mentioned her pride in having set up the Royal Commission into child sexual abuse, and the government's foreign policy achievements. 'Things people said couldn't be done we have done; particularly we have strengthened both our alliance with the US while taking a major stride forward in our relationship with China . . . I am confident that I leave the prime ministership having strengthened the relationship with our major partners, every one of them. I believe the work we have done in Afghanistan is something to be proud of as an Australian nation.'

One of the most moving and fair-minded parts of her speech was her tribute to the colleagues who supported her through thick and – increasingly – thin. 'When all of those that read polls and do the commentary on them were saying that there was only one logical conclusion, and that was to change the leader, my colleagues showed courage, they showed determination, they showed spine in the face of that kind of pressure. They showed conviction in our Labor project and in our Labor cause, they showed belief in the agenda of this Labor government.

'I understand that at the Caucus meeting today, the pressure finally got too great for many of my colleagues. I respect that. And I respect the decision that they have made.'

Gillard then came to the issue that, implicitly or overtly, had been front and centre throughout the whole of her prime ministership.

'I want to just say a few remarks about being the first woman to serve in this position,' she began. 'There's been a lot of analysis about the so-called gender wars. Me playing the so-called gender card because heaven knows no one noticed I was a woman until I raised it . . .

'I've been a little bit bemused by those colleagues in the newspapers who have admitted that I have suffered more pressure as a result of my gender than other prime ministers in the past, but then concluded it had zero effect on my political position or [that] of the Labor Party. It doesn't explain everything, it doesn't explain nothing, it explains some things. And it is for the nation to think in a sophisticated way about those shades of grey.

'What I am absolutely confident of is, it will be easier for the next woman and the woman after that, and the woman after that. And I'm proud of that.'

She ended with a joke: 'I would like to say . . . to my niece who is due to have a baby in July, look forward to the most meddlesome great-aunt in Australia's history. Thank you very much.'

This was a speech in which, perhaps more clearly than she had ever done, Julia Gillard expressed her view of the power she had wielded and its purpose: to get things done, to carry out practical reforms. It also delineated her approach, to keep going on the chosen path despite all that her critics could throw at her, because once she had decided on a course of action, she followed it through. Her colleagues might have wilted under all the negative pressure from the Opposition, the press, the polls: though wounded she remained standing, and when she had to go, she accepted her colleagues' verdict with courage and grace. She spoke like the fighter she had always been, a woman who, though sometimes wrongheaded and apparently lacking an intuitive sense of what would appeal to the electorate, was never less than steadfast in her beliefs about what needed doing and in her ability to do it.

While some commentators considered that in toppling Julia Gillard Kevin Rudd had resumed his rightful place – and when he took over the prime ministership again he certainly behaved as if he had – others contrasted his approach to that of his predecessor, not always to his advantage.[1] Gillard's legislative achievements had been extraordinary, it was agreed, but she seemed unable to explain them convincingly and with authority: Rudd often failed to carry out policy and governance, but was always very good at speaking to the public and explaining what he was doing.

Perhaps this is the difference between policy and politics. Kevin Rudd was almost always more popular than Julia Gillard, and despite his chaotic unpleasantness as prime minister the first time round, his party's self-interest made them choose him again. It is a fact of human nature that people – in and out of politics – will put up with any amount of bad behaviour provided they are being given what they want.

Some of what Julia Gillard said when we spoke in May this year, though framed in the context of an impending election, now has a poignant resonance considering what happened six weeks after our meeting. 'You can look at politics in one of two ways,' she said.[2] 'Either you say, like a turbocharged version of *The Voice* or *Big Brother*, the most popular person gets to be prime minister and the second most popular is leader of the opposition, and every three years you get to choose, and maybe vote them off the island and whatever, and get a new celebrity.

'Or you say that politics is about a contending sense of values and plans.

'One of the things I say to [colleagues who are nervous about opinion polls] is that out in the big wide world, voters don't worry about them when it comes to the crunch.

'The questions they have for all politicians, not just on the Labor side, are: Do you have a sense of purpose, and what are you in politics for? Are you in it for yourself, or in it for me? Are you in it to do something for the nation, or for self-aggrandisement?

'And if for any political party the most popular person is leader simply because they are the most popular, well . . . I have always believed that chasing popularity is the death of purpose.'

NOTES

CHAPTER 1

1 Julia Gillard interview with Jacqueline Kent, 7 May 2013.

2 Megalogenis, George, 'Too much Tony, too little Julia', *The Australian*, 28 July 2010.

3 Green, Antony 'How Australia Voted', Antony Green's Election Blog, 20 September 2010, at blogs.abc.net.au/antonygreen/2010/09/how-australia-voted.html.

4 Tony Windsor quoted, Daley, Gemma, 'How Julia Gillard keeps her government in power', *Australian Financial Review*, 27 December 2012, at afr.com/p/national/how_julia_gillard_keeps_her_government_kDHcgvhQiMrCWhzemm0JzO.

5 Doughney, James, 'Pokies reforms explained: how good intentions were derailed', The Conversation, 24 January 2012, at theconversation.com/pokies-reforms-explained-how-good-intentions-were-derailed-5001.

6 'How Julia Gillard keeps her government in power', op. cit.

7 Evershed, Nick, 'Was Julia Gillard the most productive prime minister in Australia's history?' *The Guardian*, Datablog, 28 June 2013, at guardian.co.uk/news/datablog/2013/jun/28/australia-productive-prime-minister.

CHAPTER 2

1 Gillard interview, 7 May 2013, op. cit.

2 Gillard, Julia, Australian Industry Group speech, 20 December 2007.

3 Gillard, Julia, Gough Whitlam Oration, 31 March 2011, at whitlam.org/the_program/gough_whitlam_oration/oration.

4 Gillard interview, 7 May 2013, op. cit.

5 Turnbull, Malcolm, 'What's Wrong with the Resource Super Profit Tax', MacolmTurnbull.com.au, 10 May 2010, at malcolmturnbull.com.au/blogs/whats-wrong-with-the-resource-super-profits-tax.

6 Keane, Bernard, and Dyer, Glenn, 'Australia: still officially the safest place for mining investment in the world', Crikey, 8 April 2013, at crikey.com.au/2013/04/08/australia-still-officially-the-safest-place-for-mining-investment-in-the-world.

CHAPTER 3

1 Jeannie Rea quoted, Matchett, Stephen, 'Gillard to pull $2.3bn of funding from unis to pay for Gonski reforms', *The Australian*, 14 April 2013, at theaustralian.com.au/national-affairs/gillard-to-pull-23bn-of-funding-from-unis-to-pay-for-gonski-reforms/story-fn59niix-1226619719867.

2 Frazer, Simon, 'Academic questions impact of university cuts', *PM*, ABC Radio, 15 April 2013, at abc.net.au/pm/content/2013/s3737408.htm.

3 Jones, Tony, 'Safeguards not met on Manus Island', *Lateline*, ABC-TV, 4 April 2013, at abc.net.au/lateline/content/2013/s3730221.htm.

CHAPTER 4

1 McKnight, David, *Rupert Murdoch: An Investigation of Political Power*, Allen & Unwin, Sydney, 2012, p. 209.

2 Ibid., p. 225.

3 Gillard interview, 7 May 2013, op. cit.

4 Ibid.

5 Summers, Anne, 'Her Rights at Work', The Looking Glass, 31 August 2012, at annesummers.com.au/speeches/her-rights-at-work-r-rated.

6 Julia Gillard quoted, 'I give as good as I get', op. cit.

7 Gillard interview, 7 May 2013, op. cit.

8 Ibid.

CHAPTER 5

1 Gillard interview, 7 May 2013, op. cit.

2 Swan, Wayne, statement, 22 February 2010, at smh.com.au/opinion/political-news/wayne-swans-official-statement-20120222-1to8e.html.

3 Kim Carr quoted, Kirk, Alexandra, 'Carr says PM not unhappy with his performance', *PM*, ABC Radio, 16 December 2011, at abc.net.au/am/content/2011/s3392225.htm.

4 Simon Crean quoted, Legge, Kate, 'Simon Crean reveals failed Labor spill months in the making', *The Australian*, 27 April 2013, at theaustralian.com.au/national-affairs/politics-news/simon-crean-reveals-failed-labor-spill-months-in-the-making/story-fn59nqld-1226630381592.

5 Gillard interview, 7 May 2013, op. cit.

6 Ibid.

7 Latham, Mark, 'Gillard right in rejecting Labor roosters', *Australian Financial Review*, 11 April 2013, at afr.com/p/opinion/gillard_right_in_rejecting_labor_ncDOev5kQ8G9J86Oy4N3BN

8 Editorial, 'For the sake of the nation, Ms Gillard should stand aside', *The Age*, 22 June 2013, at theage.com.au/federal-politics/editorial/for-the-sake-of-the-nation-ms-gillard-should-stand-aside-20130621-2006e.html.

CHAPTER 6

1 Burgess, Rob, 'Rudd's triumph of style over substance', *Business Spectator*, 27 June 2013, at businessspectator.com.au/article/2013/6/27/politics/rudd's-triumph-style-over-substance.

2 Gillard interview, 7 May 2013, op. cit.

ALSO BY JACQUELINE KENT

The Making of Julia Gillard: Prime Minister

THE FIRST BIOGRAPHY OF AUSTRALIA'S FIRST FEMALE PRIME MINISTER.

Julia Gillard has always been an exceptional figure in Australian politics, widely admired by her adversaries as well as in the electorate. And now she is also an exceptional figure in Australian history: the first woman to be this country's Prime Minister.

The path to power has been far from smooth. Gillard's career has been marked by pitched battles with jealous rivals and powerful factions. But as she herself has observed, 'I am proof that a woman can thrive in an adversarial environment.'

Drawing on interviews with her friends

and foes – and with Julia Gillard herself – award-winning biographer Jacqueline Kent gives us the first thorough account of her career before she challenged for the top job. It describes Gillard's Adelaide childhood, her time as a fiery student activist, her battles to get into Parliament and her relationships with the important men in her political life: Simon Crean, Kim Beazley, Mark Latham and Kevin Rudd.

The Making of Julia Gillard is an insightful and immensely readable account of this remarkable woman, how adversarial her environment has been and how she has thrived.

'She fascinates us, not just because she is the first to be where she is but because she is so good. This book will be eagerly devoured by those who want to know more about her.'

ANNE SUMMERS, *Sydney Morning Herald*

